Dan Cate
for you.

OWN THE
MAP

Marketing Your Law Firm's
Address Online

Conrad P. Saam

CONRAD SAAM

AMERICAN**BAR**ASSOCIATION

Law Practice Division

CONTENTS

ABOUT THE AUTHOR

After leading marketing efforts for Avvo, Conrad Saam founded Mocking-bird, an online marketing agency focused exclusively on the legal sector. Conrad is the author of *The FindLaw Jailbreak Guide*, he is a Google Small Business Advisor, and he has held various American Bar Association (ABA) Law Practice Management roles. A semi-professional bridge arsonist, Conrad enjoys publishing cease and desist letters from unscrupulous legal marketing vendors. He once bought the keyword "mesothelioma lawyer" for $4.76. Conrad is the proud owner of Zippy, the first and only chicken to be awarded the Lawyers of Distinction Top 10% Award.

ACKNOWLEDGMENTS

A week after my fifth high school reunion, I received a handwritten card in the mail from the parent of one of my classmates. This book, more than anything else, is a result of that note. My classmate's mother, Mrs. Perone, was responding to the personal write-up I had submitted for our reunion. Instead of the typical "this is where I went to college, this is what I majored in, and this is where I'm working now," my where-are-they-now blurb was an ironic, slightly inappropriate—albeit eloquent—anecdote that married the past and the future. Mrs. Perone wrote to me, "You've always been so different. I know you'll do something great in the future . . . perhaps become an author." At that moment, I promised myself, and tacitly, Mrs. Perone, that one day I would indeed become a published author. Never underestimate the impact your actions might have. And in this age of email, texts, and social media posts, try sending a handwritten note. It might make a much bigger impact that you ever imagined.

I'd also like to thank Richard O'Hara, whose 9th grade English class I hated at the time but actually introduced me to the delight of artful writing, and my ABA Editor, Sarah Craig, whose patience and professionalism I neither earned nor deserved.

INTRODUCTION

Forty-three percent of legal clients select their attorney based on proximity.[1] Let that sink in.

Nearly half the people who seek legal counsel choose a lawyer based primarily on where that attorney happens to be physically located. These are people who frequently are facing serious issues that have massive personal and financial ramifications: fighting for access to their children; waging a *David versus Goliath* battle against a large insurance company; managing their son's embarrassment when he grew breasts after taking Risperdal.

Address matters most. Not the diploma on the wall, nor the sheen of the mahogany desk, nor the expansiveness of the lobby. What matters most for people who are choosing a lawyer is the geographic convenience of a lawyer's location. It's time for attorneys and law firm marketers to understand that office location in relation to prospective clients is a marketing asset—or a liability—that must be leveraged to maximize effectiveness across all marketing efforts.

The clear consumer preference for proximity as a key factor when choosing a lawyer is demonstrated in search result data. The preference is clearly driven by the widespread adoption of smartphones—people are searching for "pizza restaurants near me," "ATMs near me," and, yes, even "divorce lawyer near me." The following graph shows Google Trends search data for queries that include the phrase "near me" in the legal category:

---

1. This is taken from a 2017 Google study on consumer behavior in the legal industry and was the most striking data point shared by Google during our Legal Connect with Google events held from 2017 to 2018 across the country.

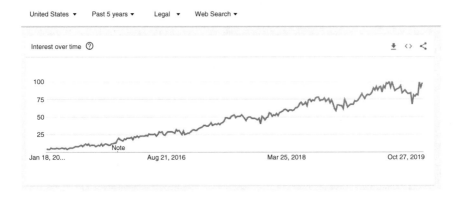

If done well, marketing campaigns, including search engine optimization, pay-per-click, remarketing, email, and social media, employ a precise local facet that is the key to success and profitability for businesses. Precision location targeting through these various channels transforms advertising costs into marketing investments. This book takes a detailed trip into the mind of the prospective legal customer. And in legal, that customer is almost always local. The book highlights actionable marketing tactics that successful law firms employ to capitalize on the consumer preference for the convenience of location.

I
BUSINESS REPORTING
AND GOOGLE ANALYTICS

Marketing "how to" books usually save the topic of reporting for last, like a report card that comes at the end of the school year. However, I want to push business reporting to the very front and center of this book to serve as a reminder that the overriding priority of online marketing is to serve the business. Too frequently, all of the metrics, dashboards, and data that are delivered by vendors and tools miss this fundamental point. Online marketing doesn't matter at all if it doesn't serve the needs of the business. In this book, that business is a law firm. Even for law firms, to be worthwhile, online marketing must generate customers at a profitable cost per client.

Understanding the terminology and fundamentals of what is reported by various online tools and marketing vendors can help lawyers focus on what needs to be optimized—and what they can safely ignore.

Google Analytics

A carefully configured Google Analytics account is the perfect tool for tracking and evaluating the effectiveness of a law firm's online marketing initiatives. Google Analytics is a free, widely used, extremely flexible system that's employed for millions of websites. It is built for a wide array of different websites, from e-commerce to publishers, and for small businesses like law firms. When configured correctly, almost all online marketing results can be evaluated through a Google Analytics account. From a managerial

1

perspective, it is very important to have a single interface (dashboard) where you can evaluate the efficacy of your marketing investment. Google Analytics is that solution.

The vast majority of functionality in Google Analytics is ignored in the following overview. That's because much of that functionality is irrelevant to a localized, service-based business like legal. The focus of this section of the chapter is highlighting the Google Analytics reporting elements that are specifically relevant to law firms.

Note that the primary limitation of Google Analytics is that it reports exclusively on user behavior on a single website. You can't use your Google Analytics account to monitor marketing tactics that aren't based on your website (like advertising on Avvo, Yelp, TV, or in the phone book, for example)—although a good law firm business reporting system can and should include it all. Performance on a third-party site, in which a law firm is dependent on the self-reported results of its advertising vendors, can be hard to accurately evaluate for apples-to-apples comparisons. In their attempt to win more advertising dollars and retain their legal customers, third parties are prone to liberal stretching of data and definitions. For example, Yelp counts a consumer view of a law firm photo on Yelp as a "lead."[1]

Taking Action

A sophisticated, comprehensive reporting system is foundational to making smart and quantitative decisions about marketing investments. However, a reporting system is only one piece of the overall puzzle. As important is the regular and deliberate review of online reporting data to evaluate the efficacy of different marketing channels. Reviewing online reporting data needs to lead to actionable changes in marketing tactics—halting poorly performing marketing channels or doubling down on an investment in channels that are performing very well.

The review frequency for marketing activity is determined by basic statistical fundamentals: you need a sample size that's large enough on which to base a smart, math-based decision for any given channel. If you review data too

---

1.   Conrad Saam, *Yelp's Grossly Inflated "Lead" Reporting*, MOCKINGBIRD MARKETING (Jun. 27, 2016), https://mockingbird.marketing/yelps-grossly-inflated-lead-count. Yelp's "customer leads" include mobile check-ins, mobile calls, user-uploaded photos, directions, map views, clicks to a website, Yelp bookmarks, deals sold, and messages as "leads." This is extremely misleading. Compare the value of a simple click to a website as a "lead" versus an inbound phone call to a law firm.

frequently, you make underinformed decisions. But, not reviewing marketing performance regularly enough means that you will continue to invest in poorly performing marketing tactics . . . leading to an ongoing drip-drip-drip of money bleeding out of the firm's bank account. In general, we recommend following these admittedly very general guidelines for setting up a regular quantitative review of marketing performance:

- A quarterly review for firms that spend less than $2,000 monthly
- A monthly review for firms that spend between $2,000 and $30,000 per month
- A weekly review of channels that spend more than $30,000 per month[2]

A High-Level Tour of the Google Analytics Interface

There are literally hundreds of thousands of ways to view data in Google Analytics. The product is built for a large variety of use cases, from large online retailers to small photo-sharing blogs. What follows is a high-level overview to help you navigate Google Analytics from the perspective of a law firm.[3]

Google Analytics groups site traffic into Channels. You can look at the behavior and performance of search engine optimization (SEO) traffic and compare it to traffic from social media, for example. A variety of default Channels are available automatically:

- **Direct**[4]: Direct traffic represents users who directly load a website. For example, a user who types **mockingbirdmarketing.com** into the browser shows up in the Direct channel. A user who accesses Amazon.com through a bookmark saved in their web browser also appears in the Direct channel. For law firms, Direct traffic usually represents firms that have a strong brand. Offline branding

---

2. Extremely large spends (more than $30,000 per month) might warrant a daily review, but this is the exception rather than the rule. Reviewing any marketing performance more frequently than weekly completely skips the weekly cadence of interest in hiring lawyers: trends show high interest in hiring lawyers on weekdays and low interest on weekends. Any analysis that doesn't take this cycle into account is potentially incomplete.

3. The Google Analytics interface is continuously being improved and updated. In this book, we discuss examples of features that are available as of the publication date.

4. Frequently referred to as *direct load.*

campaigns, like on TV or radio, often correlate to an increase in Direct traffic.

- **Referral**: Google Analytics uses a lexicon that confuses many law firms. A primary channel in Google Analytics is the Referral channel, which tracks referrers. In the Google Analytics world, this refers to traffic that comes from other sites that link to your site. For example, if SearchEngineLand.com links to my brilliant article about link spam analysis on the Mockingbird Marketing blog, traffic that comes from that link is grouped into the Referral channel. Note the potential for immense confusion within law firms, where a *referral* typically is a prospective case that is referred by another law firm or contact based on a preexisting personal relationship.[5] The potential for confusion with Google Analytics referrals is significant. It is extremely important for law firms to continue to correctly report on, and attach a high importance to, business that's driven by these all-important human referral relationships.[6]

- **Social**: Referral traffic from social media sites is segmented out into the Social channel. For law firms, this is predominantly Facebook, Yelp, Twitter, and LinkedIn. We will go much deeper into link-building in a later chapter. However, traffic driven by social media often is a result of a content strategy of highly creative, linkworthy content. In the following example, Google Analytics shows a firm that has an extremely successful YouTube channel, which drives clicks back to the firm's website. Note that although these users might or might not actually be looking to hire an attorney, this traffic is reflective of highly creative content, and it frequently shows up as spikes in traffic from the Social channel.

---

5.   While we are on the topic of personal referrals . . . Although this is a book about online marketing, note that the power and value of interpersonal relationships in driving business will continue to remain very strong. A firm's overall marketing strategy can and should continue to develop (both online and offline) real-life, human relationships as a huge driver of business. There is simply nothing more relevant to local marketing than a referral from someone in town.

6.   An accurate and sophisticated reporting infrastructure will correctly identify which online marketing channels are used to drive inquiries to the business. This reporting infrastructure obviates the need to ask prospects, "*How did you hear about us?*" (An obnoxious and invasive interruption to the onboarding process.) The only exception here is the importance of asking about personal referrals, which is completely appropriate and, if handled well, not at all invasive. You can use this simple question during intake: "*I just wanted to ask if you got our name from anyone. . . . I always like to send a personal thank-you when one of our friends recommends us.*"

Social Network ?	Sessions ? ↓
1. YouTube	**3,572** (95.89%)
2. Facebook	**83** (2.23%)
3. Twitter	**30** (0.81%)
4. LinkedIn	**28** (0.75%)
5. Glassdoor	**4** (0.11%)

- **Organic Search:** Google categorizes unpaid traffic from search engine results pages as Organic Search.[7] Search nerds also refer to this as *natural search*, or simply *SEO*. Note that the Organic Search channel includes the subset of traffic that's generated by the Local Search category—that is, mapped results. Local Search runs on an entirely different algorithm than Organic Search, and it requires entirely different marketing tactics. Local Search also is highly effective at generating business for law firms. Because of this, it is important to track traffic from Local Search individually; we go into how to do this by using UTM parameters in the chapter on Local Search. (UTM parameters refer to parts of a URL that identify the marketing campaign that refers traffic to a website.)
- **Email:** This is traffic to a website that originates in email. This can include traffic from a firm's email newsletter and traffic from any emailed links, such as from gmail.com or mail.yahoo.com.
- **Paid Search:** This channel captures paid search traffic (and in many cases, the specific keyword that was used) from paid search campaigns. Google and Bing make it easy to automatically categorize their campaigns as Paid Search through the use of auto-tagging. You can include other paid channels, like Facebook Ads, in the Paid Search channel if you manually apply UTM tracking codes.[8]

---

7.   Google Analytics does not include search traffic from DuckDuckGo, by default.

8.   To go really deep on this topic, see https://www.optimizesmart.com/understanding -channels-in-google-analytics.

- **Display:** Attorneys are increasingly using the Display channel. Display includes traffic that's generated by classic banner advertising, which typically is a brand-building exercise. Like Paid Search, you can configure the Display channel for advertisers in addition to Google by customizing UTM codes.
- **Other:** This is the catchall for everything that doesn't fit into a predefined category. Traffic generated for URLs that have a UTM code that lack a "medium" show up as (**not set**) in the Other channel.

One of the most valuable features in Google Analytics is the ability to view all the reports by an individual segment. This feature filters reports to include only traffic from the selected marketing channel or from a combination of attributes (such as first time visitors or people from Atlanta) or channels. You access this functionality at the top of the Google Analytics interface; it defaults to **All Users**. You can add a segment to compare how a portion of the traffic compares against overall traffic, or isolate a single marketing channel. For example, if a firm wants to assess the effectiveness of its SEO agency's work, it can simply segment Google Analytics traffic by Organic Search to separate the analysis of SEO performance from other marketing channels. In Google Analytics parlance, segments can be configured beyond just marketing channel. Segments can include other information about groups of site visitors. For example, you can create a segment of visitors in your city who came to the site from the marketing channel SEO, and who have never been to the site before. This segment, for example, is particularly effective in evaluating the efficacy of your SEO program in driving new, prospective clients to your firm.

Google Analytics by Date Range

Google Analytics displays website traffic over various time intervals. You can modify the intervals by adjusting the date in the upper right corner of the interface:

Intervals also can group traffic by day, week, or month. Website traffic to law firms tends to follow a weekly cycle, with very low traffic on weekends and higher traffic on weekdays. You can avoid the cardiogram-looking results of this traffic pattern (in which traffic drops predictably during the weekend, and then spikes on weekdays) by grouping traffic by week.

This:

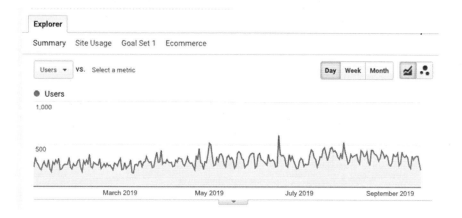

Becomes this:

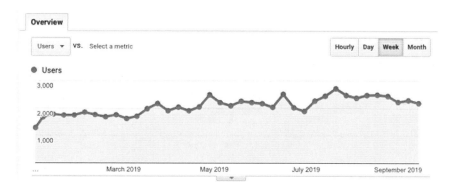

Legal website traffic—and therefore, demand for legal services—also follows an annual pattern: overall lower interest during the summer months and a more dramatic drop between Thanksgiving and New Year's. Some specific practice areas show other patterns—divorce law traffic cruelly sees demand surge by 40% around Valentine's Day[9] and DUI defense predictably peaks Saturday through Monday and around holidays like St. Patrick's Day.

Saved Reports and Dashboards

It's easy to feel overwhelmed by the sheer volume of reports that are available in Google Analytics. As already discussed, most of these reports are immaterial to the marketing of a law firm. Homing in on the reports that really matter is very important. Also, instead of struggling to regenerate the same useful reports from scratch each time, either use the Save functionality, or create a dashboard to organize a series of key reports. You can save every single report that you generate or view in Google Analytics.

You can then access the report through **Customization** in the left menu:

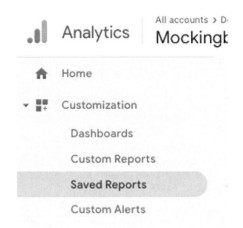

---

9.   *Valentine's Day Heartbreak! Divorce Surges Around Day of Romance*, Avvo Stories (Feb. 10, 2011), http://stories.avvo.com/media-resources/press-releases/valentines-day-heartbreak -divorce-surges-around-day-of-romance.

Reporting Vernacular

Here's a list of common terms you'll see in Google Analytics:

- **Session:** A session is a set of actions that result from a single visit to a website.[10] A single user might generate multiple sessions, for example, if she returns to the website the following day. Said differently, a session is a container of actions a user takes during one visit to the website. Sessions expire by either a time-based definition or by a change in campaigns. Default time-based settings are 30 minutes of inactivity or midnight. For example, one user who returns to view a site after their hour-long lunch break would count as two sessions.

- **Bounce rate:** Bounce rate is the percentage of sessions that view one page on a website and then leave. Traditional publishing websites (which generated revenue through display advertising) worked very hard to reduce bounce rate because it affected revenue (fewer pageviews = fewer ads served = fewer advertising dollars generated). In the early 2000s, the term *sticky* came into vogue and was used to describe the design of sites that deliberately encouraged multiple pageviews. However, in legal, these metrics of traffic quality don't necessarily translate directly. For example, a session that sees one page, decides to call the lawyer, and then leaves the site would be considered a bounce. But that's exactly what law firms want to happen. So, contrary to conventional wisdom, a law firm website with a high bounce rate is not necessarily a bad thing. Google fully understands this dynamic.[11]

- **Pageview:** This is the number of pages viewed by all visitors during a specified time frame.

- **Pageviews per session:** This number is pageviews divided by sessions. Similar to bounce rate, this metric frequently has been cited by publishing websites who seek to maximize the number of ads displayed in a session as an indicator of traffic quality. However, the same logic does not apply to law firms. Having a high number

---

10. At one time, sessions might have been referred to as "hits," which is both confusing and inaccurate. Avoid online marketing vendors who use the word "hits" unless they're discussing the Eagles, Queen, or Neil Young, and "hits" is immediately preceded by the word "Greatest."

11. Barry Schwartz, *Google vs. Moz On Clicks Influencing Search Ranking*, SEARCH ENGINE ROUND TABLE (March 24, 2016), https://www.seroundtable.com/googles-andrey-lipattsev-moz-s-rand-ishkin-discuss-clicks-influencing-ranking-21826.html.

of pageviews per session is a poor metric for law firm traffic quality. The perfect situation is a visitor who sees just one page and is so inspired by the lawyer and content that they pause or stop their web search and inquire with the law firm. This is a single pageview—technically, a bounce—and yet, the user responded to what the website was designed for: to deliver compelling content and trigger contact by the user. Despite this, many SEO agencies (especially those who don't specifically focus on the legal industry) continue to push pageviews per session as an important SEO ranking factor.

- **User:** A user[12] is an individual person who views a website. A single user might engage in multiple sessions to a website. It's not quite that straightforward anymore, though. Users used to be identified by cookies on the computer from which they visited. But in that model, you might have multiple individuals registering as a single user—say, family members who all use the family computer to shop at Amazon.com. Google now uses a variety of signals, including login information, to identify individual users, even across different computers. For example, Bill is logged into his Gmail account on both his phone and his work computer. Google Analytics correctly identifies him as a single user on these two different devices. This increases the accuracy of your marketing data—Bill's two different logins are not confused as different people, but instead are tracked as a single returning user.

Tracking Advertisers

Google Analytics helps marketers analyze the performance of traffic that's generated from advertising by grouping traffic from predefined sources into segments. For example, let's say a law firm starts a paid advertising campaign that uses banner advertisements on a local website, SanJose.com. The firm must know how much traffic the banners generate and, ideally, whether the traffic from those banners generates inquiries to the law firm (conversions) and, ultimately, customers. Later, we'll dive into mechanisms for calculating cost per customer; for now, know that these basic business metrics help the firm assess whether it should continue with SanJose.com or move its marketing investment elsewhere.

---

12. Sometimes referred to as *unique users* or *UUs*.

Advertiser Vendor Reporting

Online marketing vendors are all too happy to submit their own, customized reports. This, of course, places the fox firmly in the henhouse. Vendors who generate their own reports have free reign to exaggerate, confuse, mislabel, or deliberately obfuscate and muddle data to hide a lack of results. Law firms should insist that vendors use Google Analytics, because the data doesn't lie.

Another tactic some advertising vendors use to hide data is to build additional websites so the traffic can't be analyzed in the client's existing Google Analytics account. Additional websites might make sense if an existing website is horrendously outdated or poorly designed, but there are few other benefits. Explanations that data-sharing is proprietary or not possible, or that *"we can't share this because we'd be exposing you to the data for all of our other clients"* are simply poor attempts to hide poor performance, and it shouldn't be tolerated. We put a man on the moon 50 years ago; we can certainly make data available in a free, easy-to-use tool today.

Google Analytics enables sophisticated, highly targeted tracking through the use of UTM codes,[13] which append tracking information through a parameter added to the end of a URL. In plain English, the following two URLs are identical, but the parameter (which starts at the question mark [?]) helps Google segment out traffic from the second URL as traffic that comes from SanJose.com:

http://Fuzzybunnyslippers.com

http://Fuzzybunnyslippers.com /?utm_ source=SanJose&utm_medium= Banner&utm_campaign=FreeBook&utm_content=AdB

Look carefully and you'll see that there's even more information packed into the end of that parameter. Not only did it come from "San Jose," but it was for a "Free Book" campaign. Furthermore, the user clicked on a banner advertisement, and it even calls out which banner ad—in this case, "Ad B."

---

13. For the history nerds . . . UTM is an acronym for Urchin Tracking Module. Urchin was a small website analytics provider in the early 2000s—a period where there were approximately 20 different vendors vying for market share in the online analytics space. Urchin was purchased by Google in 2005. Instead of requiring all legacy installations of Urchin to be recoded under a more Googley (yes, it's a word in Mountain View) moniker, Google engineers wisely preserved the existing UTM approach.

Armed with this information, advertisers can isolate at every level which publishers, campaigns, ad formats, and even individual advertisements are most effective. Combine this with advanced conversion tracking, and a firm can identify exactly which marketing investments generate clients and which torch the partners' kids' college fund.

There are five different elements of a UTM code:

- **Source:** This is the referring advertising partner—say, Facebook or Avvo or Yelp.
- **Medium:** This is the type of marketing channel—pay-per-click (PPC), banners, social media, email newsletters, etc.
- **Campaign:** This identifies what campaign is being run—for a retail store, it might be "Grand Opening" or "Back to School." For legal, it might be practice area–specific, like "Car Accidents."
- **Term:** This is used exclusively for keyword-based advertising. It brings the actual keyword the user clicked into the Google Analytics system.
- **Content:** This optional field is used to differentiate ads within the same campaign. In our San Jose banner example, you would use **Campaign Content** to differentiate between banners of different sizes, or banners that have different imagery and calls to action.

Note that UTM codes are case-sensitive. The following example shows the importance of consistency in the implementation of UTM codes. Because of inconsistent tagging approaches, traffic from Twitter is split into three different channels for this law firm:

☐	1.	Twitter	**694** (70.89%)
☐	2.	twitter.com	**284** (29.01%)
☐	3.	twitter.com\	**1** (0.10%)

Many large advertising platforms have adapted their own reporting to make it extremely easy to append UTM codes through auto-tagging—essentially appending what they believe the appropriate UTM parameters should be. The Google Ads platform does this, for example. Note that if you rely on an advertiser's auto-tagging functionality, you are subject to their whims regarding how that information is presented in your Google Analytics interface.

Configuring UTM Codes for Local Search

UTM codes work for both paid and unpaid campaign tracking. A particularly useful implementation of UTMs is to use them to track the success of Google Maps results to actually generate traffic. (Remember, we don't care about rankings; we only care whether those rankings actually generate traffic, which generates inquiries, which generates business.) By appending a UTM code to the URL submitted to Google My Business, we can track clicks directly from those mapped results to the law firm's website. This has become increasingly important as Google Local results continue to drive more and more business to law firms, given their prominent placement on the SERPs.

In the following Google Analytics reports, by properly isolating traffic from Google maps by using UTM parameters, we have configured the firm's reporting infrastructure to track the firm's traffic coming from its Las Vegas office's Local Search presence.

	Campaign	Users ⬍ ↓	Users
		396 % of Total: 18.22% (2,173)	**396** % of Total: 18.22% (2,173)
	1. ■ GMB-Vegas	**228**	**57.58%**

UTM codes help provide a framework for evaluating the cost-effectiveness of marketing investments. For example, a firm can legitimately ask whether the $5,000 it spent on Local SEO was worth an additional 80 visitors per month. The same approach can apply to evaluating paid advertising or determining whether the effort invested in channels like social media is worth the results.

Remember, Google Analytics is a comprehensive, free tool. It has open-data APIs that enable it to bring in every significant and necessary element for running a law firm's marketing, just like an MBA would. Any online marketing vendor who is incapable of, or who refuses to, provide full transparency through Google Analytics is either hiding something or is incompetent.

Often, the biggest barriers to utilizing Google Analytics is having continued access to the back end of your website to install tracking scripts, as well as modifying contact forms to track submissions, link clicks, button presses, etc. Google created Google Tag Manager to solve this very issue. Once you've installed two pieces of the Google Tag Manager code in specific areas of your website, you no longer need back-end access to set up event tracking, link tracking, or thank-you page visits. All of this can be done off-site through Google Tag Manager.

Think of Google Tag Manager as a simple container for all your tracking pixels and scripts, helping you manage everything from one place instead of editing your website's theme files or plug-ins. You can simply add your call-tracking scripts, Bing UET[14] tags, Facebook pixels, Google Analytics code, and everything else to a single, organized Google Tag Manager account. It's quite simple, yet extremely powerful.

Conversions

The primary function of a law firm website is to generate inbound inquiries from prospective clients. These inquiries ("conversions," in Google Analytics parlance) come in four—and only four—different methods:

- Phone calls
- Form fills
- Chat
- Text (yes, seriously)

The role of a well-designed site in encouraging conversions is *not* to deliver prospects in the method favored by the law firm. Instead, it is to make it as convenient and inviting as possible for the prospect to contact the law firm through the method in which he or she is most comfortable at that moment. And while a lawyer might believe that she closes better on the phone, not everyone wants to talk to a lawyer right away. Perhaps the prospect is suing their employer and researching from the office, or leaving her husband and researching at home while the kids are around. Wise firms embrace all four flavors of inbound inquiries—which encourages more and more business.

---

14.   Microsoft Bing's tagging methodology.

Conversion goals can be utilized on a variety of different marketing channels. For example, use conversion tracking to see whether email newsletters do anything at all to drive business. A sophisticated tracking infrastructure will show if someone not only clicks through to the website, but also if that person ultimately contacts the firm via form fill, chat, text, or phone, or dials directly through to the law firm through a tracking number embedded in email. Offline channels like TV, radio, and billboards incorporate sophisticated tracking numbers from the reporting infrastructure to cross-compare marketing efficacy across multiple offline and online channels. An extremely sophisticated marketing reporting infrastructure accurately contrasts data both from online and offline channels to maximize the overall effectiveness of a marketing spend.

Phone Calls (And Obnoxious, Ineffectual Front Desks)

Phone calls are the classic, tried-and-true contact method. To encourage phone calls, the firm's local number should be prominently available in the upper-right side of the website's header. On a mobile device, phone numbers should be sticky—i.e., they should persist on the screen (typically at the top or bottom), regardless of what the user is reading. This phone number should be functional—when selected on a mobile device, the device should actually dial the number. There have been numerous debates around the value of a 1-800 or 1-888 number for law firms. My extremely strong bias is that the local number is a strong indicator to the prospect that they are speaking with a local firm.

Note one blindingly obvious problem with phone calls: there must be someone to answer the phone. And that person must be empathetic, professional, and knowledgeable. Too many successful marketing campaigns funnel promising prospects to unanswered phones or to rude, overworked, unavailable, or uncaring front desk staff.

Almost as bad is if the prospect gets voicemail. In the prospect's current mind frame of "*I want something, and I want it now,*" that voicemail rarely is left—the prospect simply moves on to the next Google listing.

A study I conducted for the American Bar Association (ABA) showed less than 10% of prospects with tenable cases actually got to speak with an attorney on their first call.[15] And while lawyers may not *want* the distraction

---

15. Conrad Saam, *ABA Benchmark Study on Law Firm Intake Process*, Law Technology Today (Feb. 1, 2016), https://www.lawtechnologytoday.org/2016/02/benchmark-law -firm-intake.

of regular interruptions by tire-kicking strangers, the market certainly favors those who are willing to interrupt their day to compassionately speak with a prospective client.

A great way to assess prospective clients' experience when they call your firm is to conduct mystery calls to the firm. Lawyers can pose as a prospect, fabricate a plausible matter, and shop their own firm to get a sense of the experience a prospective client receives. Is the front desk compassionate? Professional? Detailed? Did they put the caller on hold multiple times? Did they offer their name and ask for the caller's name? Try dialing during lunch to see whether anyone picks up at all. Does the intake explain basic information around pricing? Does the firm schedule a follow-up next step? Fixing a poor front desk experience can be the most cost-effective marketing investment a firm can make. Another approach to improving the initial customer experience for new clients is to review and evaluate recordings of inbound phone calls with front desk staff. It seems obvious, but far too many intake specialists fail to consistently deliver along some basic metrics:

1. Did they use the law firm's name in their greeting?
2. Did they confirm or get a good call-back number in case of a disconnect?
3. Did they ask for the caller's name and use it during the conversation?
4. Did they introduce themselves and their role?
5. Were they empathetic?
6. Was the caller put on hold? How many times? For how long?
7. Were there clear next steps?

For firms who don't have around-the-clock phone staffing, it is worth pausing as much advertising as possible outside of office hours. Or lunch hours. Or the Michigan/Ohio State game. Different advertising platforms frequently have functionality known as dayparting and weekparting, in which advertising is activated based on a set schedule, like setting a schedule for a thermostat. It simply doesn't make sense to invest heavily in advertising during hours in which there is a low probability of conversion. Another approach is to use a call answering service for either overflow or off-hours calls.

Form Fills

Not all prospects are eager to get on the phone, but they often are more than willing to fill in a short online form. This is especially true in highly confidential issues like divorce or criminal defense. No one wants to call a divorce lawyer from the home phone or talk with an employment discrimination lawyer from the confines of an office cubicle.

A standard rule of thumb for online form fills is to require a very small amount of information—name, contact details (phone *and* email), and an optional description of the issue should suffice. Many law firms make the mistake of using form fills to vet prospects. Long, intricate, detailed online forms are a barrier. The longer and more convoluted the form is, the more it will discourage people from submitting inquiries. The vetting process is best handled after a contact has been submitted. It's better to have more inquires to weed through than a small number of highly qualified inquiries.

Submissions from online form fills should go directly to an email that is actively monitored. They should be responded to as expediently as possible. They also should be backed up on a database attached to the website, to record a history of form fill submissions if something goes wrong with email (say, the forms fills are erroneously moved to a spam folder). For sites built on WordPress, you can do this by using Contact Form 7 and the plug-in Advanced CF7 DB. Other common WordPress contact forms, like Gravity Forms and Ninja Forms, have these databases built in. Although this might sound like an unnecessary step, it is always important to do it. There have been far too many cases of inquiries via form fill that never end up on an attorney's desk for a variety of different technical and managerial issues (e.g., Jane left the firm, but her email was the only one the form sent leads to—I've seen that happen more than once).

Online form fills are notorious targets for spam submissions (expect lots of SEO and PPC "experts" submitting free SEO audits through forms, for example). It is impossible to manually eliminate spam solicitations submitted through form fills, but a well-configured form can greatly reduce computer-generated spam through the implementation of honeypots and spam-fighting plug-ins like Akismet and WordPress Zero Spam. Furthermore, it might be worth installing a security plug-in to completely block specific IP addresses or ranges of IP addresses from even reaching your site before they have a chance to send bogus contact form submissions.

Chat

Many law firm websites use third-party chat services to convert someone who is "just browsing" into a prospect. The chats electronically gather information, which is submitted to the attorney via email. In many cases, artificial intelligence has become so effective that computer-driven chat is almost indistinguishable from "chatting" with an actual human. Chat vendors typically charge per chat, and the price range typically is $8 to $22 per chat depending on practice area.

This performance-based pricing approach, while seemingly appealing to law firms, has led to extremely aggressive implementations of chat by many vendors. Specifically, many chats automatically trigger a full website takeover, hiding all content and forcing users to engage with the chat. These "interstitials" automatically launch after a set period of time (typically, 7 seconds), hide all other forms of conversion (phone and form fill), and are designed to funnel as many users as possible into engaging with chat. A much more user-centric approach is to configure chat windows to be user-initiated instead of thrusting them in the face of every visitor to your website.

In January 2017, Google announced an algorithm update that specifically penalizes sites that employed aggressive interstitials on mobile devices. In reconfiguring chat implementations to adhere to new Google best practices, some chat implementations on mobile devices now simply mask the top and bottom portion of a website with user-initiated chat. Although this seems like a reasonable solution, the top and bottom portions of a mobile-optimized webpage typically is where you'd find a firm's phone number. This sneaky implementation specifically hides the phone number from the prospect, forcing them to engage with chat instead of being able to use their phone . . . as a phone. This implementation is deliberately designed to cannibalize phone conversions—at a cost between $8 and $37 per conversion for the law firm. Choose your chat vendor extremely carefully, and ensure that you can customize the experience for your prospective clients instead of having your vendor optimize the implementation for its bottom line.

It is extremely important to note that chat is a conversion function, *not* a marketing channel. Aggressive chat salespeople frequently refer to the low cost per "lead" they can deliver, but this is erroneous and deliberately misleading. I've reviewed countless law firm reporting infrastructures that erroneously cite chat as a marketing channel. The cost of the lead really should be allocated to the marketing effort that delivered the prospect to the site. Chat is for conversions, not marketing. Calling chat a marketing channel makes as much sense as calling a telephone line or an email account (both of which can receive inbound inquires for a firm) a marketing channel.

Over the past 12 months, chat has evolved dramatically as artificial intelligence (AI) capabilities have entered chat technology. AI allows trained robotic responses instead of humans to drive much of the interaction. The obvious cost savings have generated new pricing platforms that offer either dramatically lower cost-per-chat rates or even fixed-cost pricing. Expect growth in very sophisticated hybrid chat models—with an AI robot vetting an initial prospect through chat and then transitioning that lead to a live human (via chat or phone) once a hot lead has been identified. During the next 24 months, expect the chat market to dramatically evolve as established leaders in the legal chat world, Ngage and Apex, respond to up and coming chat technology being pioneered by legal-focused startups like Gideon Software, Smith.ai, and Juvo Leads.

Text

Over the past 24 months, we have seen an increasing number of text-based inquiries to law firms. This tracking is enabled by dynamic call tracking software like CallRail, which typically forwards an inbound phone call to the firm's primary number. When that tracking number receives an inbound text, the inquiry is transcribed into an email, which is then forwarded to the law firm.

Current data[16] shows that on average, 1.2% of new inquiries are coming via text (this number is highly variable based on the law firm's practice area). At the high end of our dataset is a DUI defense firm that generates a full 3.4% of its inbound inquiries from texts. The primary challenge in managing text-based inquiries is figuring out how to handle them from an inbound perspective—who received the text (via email), and does that person respond extremely quickly and appropriately.

Conversion Tracking with Google Analytics

Because Google generates the vast majority of its revenue from advertising, it has a vested interest in ensuring that advertisers can calculate and monitor the efficacy of their advertising investment. Google Analytics handles this by associating conversion tracking with goals.

Put very simply, in Google Analytics, goals are something you want someone to do on a website. For lawyers, the only relevant goals are the four

---

16. This data was collected from a survey of more than 100 Mockingbird clients in May 2019.

conversion types—phone calls, form fills, chat, and texts. Goals are set up via a variety of different mechanisms.

A feature that I'd recommend avoiding is Google Analytics' ability to assign a dollar figure to your goals. Although this feature may be very useful in industries like retail (for example, "*if we sell a book, the average profit is $5, and therefore, the value of that sale is $5*"), there frequently is huge variability in the quality of your inquiries, as well as in the potential value of the client. This is especially true in personal injury, for example.

One issue with conversion tracking in Google Analytics is that it is extremely easy to set up various different goals. Frequently, we've seen Google Analytics accounts that have numerous different goals and conversions (and frequently they are poorly labeled). Goals and conversions might include pageviews of specific items, time-on-site "goals," and other erroneous numbers that don't affect the firm's business performance, like bounce rate. Adding all these extra goals drastically confuses the reporting. Remember, for the legal industry, the primary goal is a contact via phone, form fill, chat, or text. When viewing all the reports in Google Analytics, the extremely valuable (in fact, perhaps the most valuable) data is how each lens through which you view the data affects that primary business object: new inquiries. Extra, superfluous goals configured in Google confuse this reporting by adding goals that aren't really important to the business.

In the following example, we see how valuable it is to associate conversion data to marketing data. This is real data from a real firm, and here, we see that Organic Search generates the vast majority of this firm's inquiries. There are a couple elements to note. First, the firm has created a unique channel for Avvo. Additionally, although Organic Search may generate the vast majority of the website sessions, those sessions convert at the lowest rate (1.33%). Compare this to the custom channel the firm created for Avvo, which shows a much different conversion rate (26%). Armed with this information, the firm can answer key strategic questions, such as, "*Should our investment be redistributed elsewhere?*", "*Is our SEO agency worth our $6,000 per month investment?*", and "*Should we expand our paid search budget?*" Firms can combine, validate, or refute claims from vendor salespeople about the impact of their investments. Most importantly, firms can combine this data with cost information to create a simple cross-channel cost-effectiveness comparison.

Channel Grouping		Sessions ↓	% New Sessions	New Users	Bounce Rate	Pages / Session	Avg. Session Duration	Goal Conversion Rate	Goal Completions
		10,121 % of Total 100.00% (10,121)	82.38% Avg for View: 82.29% (0.11%)	8,338 % of Total 100.11% (8,329)	67.87% Avg for View: 67.87% (0.00%)	2.01 Avg for View: 2.01 (0.00%)	00:01:58 Avg for View: 00:01:58 (0.00%)	1.55% Avg for View 1.55% (0.00%)	157 % of Total 100.00% (157)
1.	Organic Search	9,131 (90.22%)	82.59%	7,541 (90.44%)	68.04%	2.01	00:01:58	1.33%	121 (77.07%)
2.	Direct	836 (8.26%)	80.14%	670 (8.04%)	69.02%	1.95	00:01:55	2.63%	22 (14.01%)
3.	Referral	94 (0.93%)	85.11%	80 (0.96%)	54.26%	2.56	00:02:36	4.26%	4 (2.55%)
4.	Social	33 (0.33%)	75.76%	25 (0.30%)	63.64%	2.21	00:02:13	6.06%	2 (1.27%)
5.	Avvo	23 (0.23%)	82.61%	19 (0.23%)	26.09%	0.61	00:00:16	26.09%	6 (3.82%)
6.	Paid Search	4 (0.04%)	75.00%	3 (0.04%)	25.00%	2.00	00:00:44	50.00%	2 (1.27%)

A wide array of "events" cater to all different types of business objectives for the spectrum of businesses that are served by Google Analytics. Events can include number of pages viewed, specific pages or categories viewed, actions (such as selecting **Submit** for a form fill), downloading a paper, playing a video, and so on. Although some of this data might be interesting to view, to simplify and streamline reporting, we strongly recommend tracking only events that relate to conversions: a prospective client contacting the law firm via phone call, form fill, chat, or text.

Phone Call Conversions and Call Tracking

Most law firm conversions happen offline, in the form of a phone call. Phone conversion data is handled in Google Analytics as a goal reported by a dynamic call tracking service, which displays a unique phone number to callers from a specific marketing channel. Simply put, a user who visits a site from the SEO channel will see a phone number that's viewed only by people who visit that site via SEO. Google Ads visitors get a unique phone number, Avvo visitors get their own phone number, the same with Facebook, and so on. When users dial these tracking phone numbers, they are immediately forwarded to the firm's primary number. Phone calls (along with the usual caller ID information, which often includes a caller's name, city, and phone number) to these tracking numbers can then be tracked back to their specific marketing channel.

Note that Google Ads provides call tracking numbers in which the user is encouraged to contact the advertiser directly from the ad served to a mobile device.[17] This bypasses the firm's website entirely. So, a single user may be

---

17. This is not to be confused with call-only ads, in which the user's only opportunity is to call the firm directly from an ad. These campaigns can be both extremely effective and very simple to view from a reporting perspective. Call-only ads also are a great option for law firm's that have horrendously outdated websites that convert poorly. We've successfully run call-only campaigns for solo lawyers who don't even have a website.

able to dial two different tracking numbers because of that ad—one directly from the ad, and the other if she clicks through to the firm's website. This can create confusion in tracking. The best practice here is to include two different goals in Google Analytics—one for calls directly from the ad, and the other for calls from the website.

A slightly more sophisticated approach to call tracking utilizes pools of phone numbers that are associated with a specific website for even greater detail in analyzing conversions. With phone pools, instead of associating an individual phone number with a specific marketing channel, a rotating series of numbers are shown in sequence to each website visitor. If a call comes in to a specific number within a given time period (usually, two hours), call tracking knows not only which marketing channel that user came from, but everything else about that individual user—down to the paid keywords they searched on, for example. To ensure accuracy, numbers in the pool are displayed and temporarily retired on a rotating basis. The infrastructure for call tracking pools is somewhat more expensive than basic call tracking,[18] but for sites running large PPC campaigns, this is an essential method to drill down into exactly which elements of paid campaigns are generating conversions. The following graph shows a simple example of the **CallRail Lead Attribution by Source** report, which showcases which marketing channels drive the firm's marketing success:

Leads for Aug 25, 2019 – Sep 24, 2019 Pacific Time

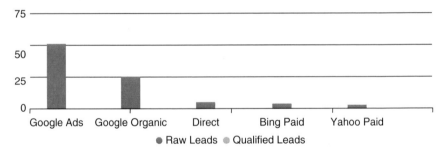

---

18.   Call tracking by using a phone number pool requires having a larger collection of phone numbers on hand. Furthermore, because each number is shown only once in a two-hour period, a site that has a large volume of traffic requires an even larger number of phone numbers in the pool—thus, expense is correlated to traffic volume.

This data drills down even deeper into individual campaigns. The next image shows Google Ads conversion numbers for different campaigns that target specific practice areas:

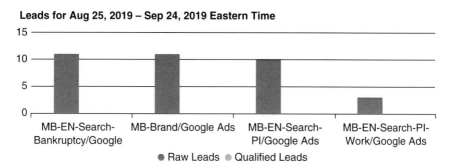

Leads for Aug 25, 2019 – Sep 24, 2019 Eastern Time

The implementation of a call tracking infrastructure is heavily complicated for firms that use multiple phone numbers on their website. This can take two forms: first, when a firm uses a 1-800 or 1-888 number, along with a local phone number. In general, this is a dated, legacy approach to marketing that encouraged phone calls from people who were wary of incurring the cost of a long-distance phone call. Thus, the term "toll-free." At this point, there is simply no conversion advantage in offering two numbers (although some firms that invest heavily in offline telephone number branding—a 1-800-LAWYER billboard, for example—might continue to use both a local and a toll-free number on their site). Note that firms who use offline branded phone numbers and who have that number displayed on their website will generate very poor-quality data when it comes to call tracking. Simply put, someone finds the firm via a Google search, lands on the site, and sees two phone numbers— one is the SEO tracking phone number, and the second is a 1-800 number. If the prospect uses the 1-800 number, she will be inaccurately not attributed to the SEO marketing channel. As such, this practice seriously degrades the quality of marketing data. The second incidence of multiple numbers on a single website is in a multi-office firm. In this case, it is imperative for all the local numbers to be listed—correctly—on the site. This is one of the key factors in Local Search performance (see chapter 3 for more information). Fortunately, around five years ago, call tracking vendors that were more sophisticated adapted to be able to implement call tracking for sites that use multiple phone numbers. However, most hand-built, hand-coded call tracking systems that rely on dedicated landing pages that have hard-coded static pages cannot.

Beware of "renting" a phone number in which you pay for access to a 1-800 vanity number in your market. You are essentially paying a temporary subscription to a marketing channel that someone else controls. This temporary benefit disappears when you stop paying that subscription. Instead, consider building out your own branded phone number with a local area code and a memorable number—206-555-5000, for example. These numbers can be acquired (at admittedly considerable expense) through phone number brokers like RingBoost.

There is another nuance that should be considered when implementing dynamic call tracking. To avoid counting every single call from the same person as an independent "conversion," call tracking should be set to report only first-time callers. This prevents repeated calls from the same needy client, the lawyer's spouse setting up lunch, or the insurance company return phone call from erroneously showing up as new inquiries and being attributed to marketing efforts. It is one of the ways low-end agencies and other vendors trick lawyers into thinking they are performing when, in fact, they are simply reporting on the same pizza delivery guy calling for directions every Friday. Smart firms look only at first-time callers and ignore reporting from vendors who don't filter out repeat callers from their reporting infrastructure. *Caveat emptor:* if the vendor doesn't specify first-time callers, they are most certainly hiding poor performance with artificially inflated "performance" numbers by reporting on every single phone call. The following image shows the simple radio button in the **CallRail** filters that you can select to report only on first-time callers:

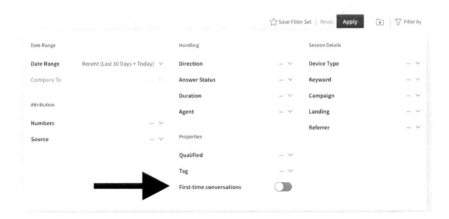

A limitation of call tracking is that many people have multiple phone numbers—a mobile number, a desk number, and a home number, for example. For the most part, a call tracking infrastructure can't find commonality between a mobile number and a work number. So, multiple calls from the same person through different lines show up as separate inquiries. One other thing to note: when initially setting up a call tracking infrastructure, the system needs to start developing a database of which numbers have already called to implement "first-time callers" reporting. Thus, the first few months will show artificially high inquiries. This data will become more accurate over time as the database of regular callers becomes more accurate.

Pulling CallRail into Google Analytics

Pulling offline conversions (phone calls and texts) into a Google Analytics interface provides a single place in which to view and contrast the ability of different marketing channels to drive conversions. Sophisticated call tracking products provide this integration ability through API. Call tracking for offline marketing tactics like radio and TV also can be pulled directly into Google Analytics by utilizing the call tracking software for offline marketing channels as well as online marketing channels. Note that the API can inadvertently generate additional fallacious sessions in the reporting. For example, in our experience with CallRail (arguably, the leading call tracking software), the API added an additional erroneous user session each time a conversion was added to the data. (What looked like an improvement in website traffic after we launched CallRail for a client was actually just the software triggering a new "computer" session.) You can handle this by filtering out sessions from CallRail's IP address. Most agencies aren't attuned to these nuances, and this same problem most likely exists with your call tracking software.

Form Fill and Chat Conversions

Conversions from form fills and chats are handled differently by triggering different events in Google Analytics. Although there are numerous different types of Google Analytics events, for law firms, events are triggered with both chat and form fill conversions. There are two primary types—one is an event that is triggered by a specific action. We trigger this when an email is sent from a form fill. (Not when the **Submit** button is pressed. We want to ensure that the actual email is sent.) The other, more common version, is a view of the thank you pageview. These pageviews are on a page that can be viewed only after a user submits a specific form and this event lets Google Analytics know that the form has been completed. Both of these events then correlate that specific conversion with all the other information collected about that session. This includes marketing channels, geographic location, paid keywords, pages visited, and so on—all key elements for marketers to evaluate the efficacy of different marketing efforts.

Eleven Very Important Google Analytics Reports

With a solid foundational understanding of how Google Analytics works, particularly as it pertains to conversions, we can dig deeper and get a feel for a small number of very insightful reports. One of the many difficulties lawyers have in dealing with Google Analytics is the sheer number of reports available. Here are 11 foundational reports to get started with. Note that some of the following reports are not necessarily out-of-the-box, preconfigured in Google Analytics; they might require significant setup and customization (for example, conversion reports incorporating third party data).

SEO Trend Analysis

"Am I winning or losing ground in the SEO wars?"

This is probably the most frequent question we field, and it usually comes under the guise of, *"my ranking for x keyword has changed,"* and *"can you get me to rank in the top 3,"* etc.[19] Using ranking reports to evaluate the efficacy of your SEO campaigns fails because ranking reports fail to take into account:

- **Personalization**—Each user gets different results based on their individual profile.
- **Location**—Search results increasingly are influenced by a user's location, which is difficult to replicate with ranking reports.
- **Volume**—Ranking reports don't take into account how many people are actually searching for a specific query.

---

19. For a long-winded diatribe against ranking reports, see Conrad Saam, *Excuse Me While I Have a Ranking Report Rant* SEARCH ENGINE LAND (Feb. 9, 2011), https://searchengineland.com/excuse-me-while-i-have-a-ranking-report-rant-64173. Although the article is dated (2011), the concepts are still very relevant.

- **Long Tail**—Mathematically, there is a much larger volume of queries in the long tail (i.e., extremely specific queries, such as "left hand turn accident on my motorcycle do I have a case" instead of "motorcycle lawyer.")
- **SERP layout**—Ranking reports don't take into account the layout of the SERP, which is now configured to prioritize local ads, and then Organic Search.

The real answer to how your site performs in SEO is to look at an overlying trend in inbound SEO traffic. SEO is a long-term play. It's an investment that continues to deliver over time. Additionally, more and more users are coming online and seeking lawyers, through more and more devices, which should show up as a slow steady increase in site traffic. We call this "up and to the right." The following graph demonstrates an "up and to the right" pattern.

First, select a long time frame of at least a year. Next, use segments, and select *only* Organic Search traffic. To generate the report, go to **Audience > Overview**. The following boring, slow, steady trend up and to the right is what you want to see. In fact, this almost-imperceptible change but week-over-week increase actually results in traffic more than doubling over a two-year period. That's real progress.

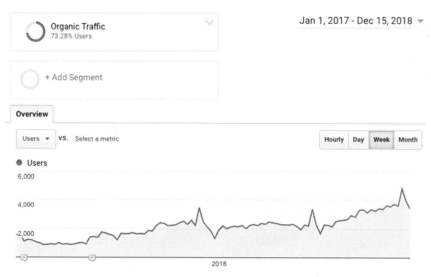

Note that almost all law firms, including the one depicted here, experience a drop in traffic during the holiday season. One way to manage this seasonality is to compare monthlong periods to your previous year by checking the **Previous year** box in the date range settings. You can isolate these data points to compare year-to-year changes—and in this case, see a 65% increase in traffic from 2017 to 2018.

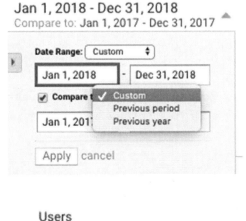

Local Traffic

"Is my website traffic coming from my geographically addressable market (i.e., in and around my office) or from Botswana, South Dakota, and Russia?"

Although an improvement in traffic ideally is what we would like to see, not all traffic is nearby. Don't forget the primary importance of proximity as it pertains to people selecting a lawyer. Traffic outside the geographic convenience of prospective clients simply isn't that useful.[20] And obviously, traffic outside of a firm's state jurisdiction is completely useless in generating business. Therefore, it's important to have a solid understanding of the geographic reach of a site's traffic.

This is very easily viewed in Google Analytics reporting through **Audience > Geo > Location**. The following map shows that a Connecticut-based personal injury firm generates the majority of its website traffic (54%, to be specific) within the firm's state.

---

20.   Note that I use the term "geographic convenience" very carefully. A small-town lawyer in Nebraska may generate business from a 30-mile to 40-mile radius, while her sister in Manhattan has clients who refuse to walk more than one city block to seek counsel.

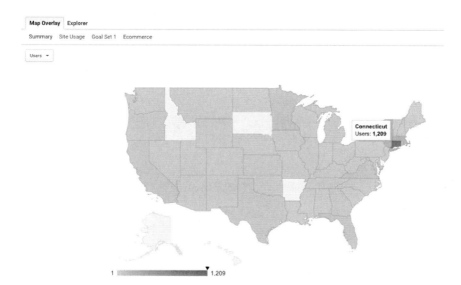

You can drill further into geographic data by looking at traffic by city or metro area within a state. In our example, we see traffic appropriately clustered around the firm's office in Hartford.

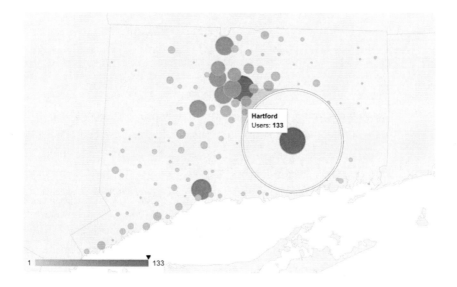

You also can create a custom segment that mimics a firm's geographic market to overlay onto all other Google Analytics reports. This is particularly important for blog-heavy sites, which typically do a good job of generating a lot of traffic outside the firm's actual market. This traffic, while flattering, simply doesn't make the phone ring.

Mobile

"Does my website perform well for users on mobile devices?"

There are countless online tools you can use to diagnose the mobile-friendliness of a website. But more important than what third-party tools tell you about your site is how it actually performs at generating traffic on mobile devices. Access mobile versus desktop versus tablet traffic data through **Audience > Mobile > Overview.**

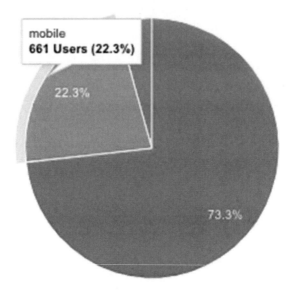

We know that over 50% of website traffic to law firms originates on mobile devices[21]—so, a site that performs far outside this average is concerning. In the example above, less than 30% of the site traffic originates from mobile devices. This begs the question, why? The answer usually is that the firm's site performs poorly in basic mobile-friendliness or site speed. Note that it is highly possible that some practice areas naturally have a low incidence of low mobile traffic—for example, law firms that focus on business. In other practices, such as criminal defense or DUI, mobile traffic is more typical.[22]

---

21.   Industry-generic studies put mobile search traffic at 52% in mid-2019. Mockingbird's legal client base mirrors those statistics. Note that "mobile" includes tablets; tablet design/portability and user behavior increasingly is not distinct from desktop (especially laptop) behavior. Read more at https://www.broadbandsearch.net/blog/mobile-desktop-internet-usage-statistics.

22.   Traffic to our agency's site, for example, typically stays north of 70% from desktops. Most lawyers aren't searching for online marketing services from their phone.

Branded vs. Unbranded Traffic

"Are users looking for me and my firm, or are they looking for a lawyer who does what I do?"

The difference here seems very subtle, although the effect on a law firm's marketing is immense. This question tries to address how much traffic arrives at the site specifically looking for information about, for example, Mary Elworth or her firm Elworth and Elworth. We call this branded traffic, and it is indicative of users who have already found their lawyer through another means and are using a site to vet that specific attorney before picking up the phone to have a conversation. This traffic is immensely valuable and tends to have a very high conversion rate. Establishing the law firm website as the primary resource for information about Mary Elworth, the lawyer, is incredibly important to Mary's business success. Many other sites that compete on name search (Yelp, Lawyers.com, etc.) frequently generate revenue by advertisers who are competing for Mary's business.

However, website sessions that arrive as branded traffic have pretty much already shortlisted Mary (if not downright selected her) before arriving at the site. This is traffic with intent to hire Mary, and it's the website's conversion to lose. Conversely, unbranded site traffic doesn't know Mary at all. They arrived at the site with a query like, "car accident lawyer, Montgomery New Jersey" or "liability for rear ended accidents NJ." Traffic from these sessions doesn't have a starting point beyond the search engines; winning these prospects generates an incremental increase in business for a law firm.

Lawyers who have a large offline presence—through reputation, TV advertising, or billboards—frequently see a large percentage of branded site traffic. In fact, branded traffic frequently directly follows patterns on offline advertising like on TV or radio.

The primary difference between branded and unbranded traffic demonstrates whether a website is incrementally growing a business instead of just reinforcing the decision of prospects who would have hired Mary anyway. You can develop an understanding of branded versus unbranded traffic by looking at which pages sessions land on: go to **Behavior** > **Site Content** > **Landing Pages**. If you are lucky and a site has been built by using good information architecture, all of the attorney profile pages will show up under a similar URL structure:

www.myfirm.com/attorneys/bill
www.myfirm.com/attorneys/mary
www.myfirms.com/attorneys/jill

You can input the common component of the URL into the search box in the **Landing Pages** report (in our example, **/attorneys/**) to show only sessions that have landed on attorney bio pages. In the next report, 5,529 out of 111,192 sessions (4.97%) landed on a lawyer's bio page.

Primary Dimension: Landing Page Other ▾			
Filter Rows. Secondary dimension ▾ Sort Type: Default ▾		/attorneys/	⚙ C
Landing Page	**Acquisition**		
	Sessions ↓	% New Sessions	New Users
	5,529 % of Total: 4.97% (111,192)	65.64% Avg for View: 79.45% (-17.37%)	3,629 % of Total: 4.11% (88,319)
1. /attorneys/	693 (12.53%)	51.37%	356 (9.81%)
2. /attorneys/▓▓▓▓▓	352 (6.37%)	68.18%	240 (6.61%)
3. /attorneys/▓▓▓▓▓	349 (6.31%)	75.07%	262 (7.22%)
4. /attorneys/▓▓▓▓▓	341 (4.17%)	71.26%	243 (6.70%)
5. /attorneys/▓▓▓▓▓	339 (6.13%)	69.62%	236 (6.50%)

Also note that this methodology does *not* include branded traffic that lands on a site's homepage. This is the difference between a user looking for "Morgan and Morgan" instead of "John Morgan." Given the wide array of different traffic that can land on the site's homepage, it's simply too far a leap to assume that all this traffic is driven by brand. Instead, we recommend looking only at traffic to specific lawyer bio pages. Reviewing a site's SEO performance by looking at this report along with the Organic Search segment is extremely insightful as to the efficacy of SEO in actually building a firm's business.

High-Converting Traffic
"Does my website generate traffic that's looking to hire a lawyer?"

By using the exact same report from the branded versus unbranded campaign, we can review the volume of traffic that starts on a practice area page of a law firm website. This type of traffic is extremely high converting—it comes from queries like "child custody lawyer Houston," and it lands directly on a firm's child custody practice page. This is a much more effective and useful method of tracking SEO success than running vanity queries around "child custody in Houston" and seeing how a site performs. And, like in the branded example, we can use the firm's URL structure to group traffic that lands on practice area pages. Returning to the previous example, this site groups practice area pages under the URL structure myfirm.com/legal-services/family-law. In this example, you'd simply enter **/legal-services/** in the search box in the **Landing Pages** report to group all traffic that lands on the firm's practice area pages. (In our example, 82 of the site's 539 visitors (15%) landed on practice area pages.)

We can drill down even further to the page level. Want more motor-cycle accident cases or wondering whether the promotion for one-hour wills worked? Simply look at inbound traffic to the respective pages for these items and see how they perform at actually generating traffic.

Is My Content Really King?

"Is my content effective? Or should I keep blogging . . . and blogging . . . and blogging . . ."

Many firms preach the widely accepted SEO rule: Content is King.[23] Teams of bored paralegals and offshore writers drip out mundane rewrites of yesterday's quasilegal "news" in a vain (and frequently ineffectual) attempt to appease content-hungry Google. Online marketing agencies blame their failings on their clients: *"You'd get more traffic if only you'd blog three times a week instead of just once."* Another inaccurate perspective perpetuated by SEO agencies is that Google simply likes sites that have fresh content, and that it's therefore important to continue to push more new content simply to maintain rankings. Although some types of sites do require fresh content for the site to be relevant (a news site, for example), this is simply not the case in the legal industry (with some obvious exceptions, such as firms that respond to legal opportunities that align with news cycles, such as product liability).

Yet, few firms have bothered to ascertain whether the blog posts they've been vomiting onto their websites do anything at all to drive business. There is a very simple way to do this. We are going to use the **Landing Pages** report again. Simply list all the URLs that have brand-new content that was writ-ten during a specific month. To give the content a fair chance to get crawled and generate traffic, go back to content written six months ago. Then, set the date range in Google Analytics to the beginning of that month to today. Next, look through the **Landing Pages** report for inbound traffic to any of the pages in that list. Are all of the pages generating traffic? How much total traffic has the new content generated? Now, ask the question, *"Is writing more content really worth the effort, or should I be doing something different*

---

23.   In 2013, I wrote a repudiation of the "content is king" fallacy that goes deeper into the history of content, the long tail, and the over-publishing that's rampant among the legal industry. If you are investing heavily in your content strategy, I recommend reading the article: Conrad Saam, *SEO Regicide: Content the King is Dead* MOCKINGBIRD MARKETING (Oct. 31, 2013), https://mockingbird.marketing/seo-regicide-content-the-king-is-dead.

with my marketing investment?" For example, if only 25% of the pages generate inbound traffic, there's a 3:1 likelihood that the next piece of content you publish will sit on your website, unseen, unloved, and utterly useless. We call this the UCR, or useless content ratio—the percentage of pages on a site that are completely useless. Add a financial perspective to this number by applying a cost per page on the content being published. Then, ask yourself whether you can generate traffic more cost-effectively by using another method, or if you are better of just finally leasing that new BMW M4 instead.

On a positive side, look at the content that *does* generate traffic. For example, I wrote a post in 2013 that outlines a business framework for analyzing the cost-effectiveness of Yelp advertising. For whatever reason, Yelp content continues to drive a large volume of our traffic. Analyzing why that specific piece of content is so effective for a site is immaterial. Instead, piggyback on the success of the most effective content as a guide for generating more content. We've built out entire niche practices of law based on content that not only generates traffic but generates business. In the case of Yelp, why not write content tangential to the original? Yelp for lawyers, Yelp's review policy, etc., and then evaluate that new content in terms of its ability to generate more traffic as well.

Which Marketing Channels Drive Traffic?
"How are people finding my site on the web?"

There is a litany of ways to drive traffic to a law firm website. Understanding which channels drive traffic is key not only to the success of your overall website, but ultimately to the efficacy of each individual marketing investment. If you spend a lot of time and money chasing likes on Facebook but you see very limited traffic to your site, is that time wasted? Begin advertising in Yelp and your firm should expect to see an influx of traffic directly from Yelp.

To view how sessions arrive at your site in Google Analytics, select **Acquisition > All Traffic > Channels**. Click the pie graph icon to see this data displayed in a pretty, colorful . . . pie graph. The following example shows a law firm that has a typical breakdown of well-balanced traffic:

Conversions

"Which marketing channels drive business inquiries?"

As discussed earlier, not all traffic behaves in a similar fashion. Prospects from some channels contact law firms at a very high rate, while others rarely, if ever, will pick up the phone and dial. For example, traffic from a properly configured branded campaign on Google Ads should convert at a much higher rate than general SEO traffic, which tends to bring in traffic much higher up in the sales funnel (i.e., people who are researching legal issues versus people who are looking to immediately hire an attorney). Understanding which marketing channels deliver a stream of potential clients is the key to understanding how to allocate your marketing effort across different channels.

In the default view (shown next) of the same **Acquisition > All Traffic > Channels** report, we review for conversions. We simply look to the far-right side of the matrix to see the number of goal completions by different channel.[24]

You can reorder this by goal conversion rate to identify the most effective conversion channels, i.e., the channels that have the highest incidence of generating an inquiry per session. Note here how SEO, although the predominant driver of traffic, actually does the worst proportionally at generating inbound inquiries.

You can dig deeper into this report to get a better feel for exactly what is working. For example, in the preceding matrix, Paid Search generated 25 leads, but was that from Google Ads, Bing, or something else? Drill into the data further by using the source link to isolate individual PPC vendors (Google Ads versus Bing Ads), or even individual campaigns.[25] In the next example, I've tried to answer the Google Ads versus Bing Ads question by looking at the data via source/medium, inputting the medium **CPC** in the search box. It now shows that although 87% of the paid search leads came from Google, the Bing traffic actually converted at a higher rate.

---

24.   Note the 3.99% contact rate for SEO traffic. This correlates directly with a study I conducted for the ABA that shows roughly 3-5 contacts per 100 sessions from SEO traffic. *Does SEO Relate to Success?* ABA Journal (Aug. 1, 2016), http://www.abajournal.com /magazine/article/numbers_law_firm_seo_success. Sites that had an aggressive approach to blog content development appeared lower than this figure in general, because the traffic was simply less qualified (i.e., not looking to hire a lawyer).

25.   You can access this same report directly from the left menu in Google Analytics: select **Acquisition > All Traffic > Source/Medium.**

Source / Medium	Acquisition			Behavior			Conversions All Goals	
	Users	New Users	Sessions	Bounce Rate	Pages / Session	Avg. Session Duration	Goal Conversion Rate	Goal Completions
	18,674	17,855	23,492	65.98%	1.94	00:01:42	9.04%	2,123
1. google / cpc	16,336	15,578	20,628	67.80%	1.86	00:01:37	8.96%	1,848
2. bing / cpc	2,332	2,277	2,864	52.86%	2.54	00:02:19	9.60%	275

How Is My Advertising Going?

"Is my paid advertising working or just burning through my kids' college fund?"

There are innumerable places for lawyers to spend their money online. Put the fundamentals of all of these reports together to track the efficacy of your marketing spends at the individual channel level. Use a combination of geographic information, conversion data, and segmentation by marketing channel (i.e., isolate traffic from your different paid marketing channels—for example, an Avvo listing, Google Ads, and Yelp) to truly analyze how your individual marketing spend is working at driving conversions from local prospects. Each paid channel should have its own segmentation and should be reviewed on a regular basis.

The Final Two Steps: Cost Per Inquiry and Cost Per Client

"How much do my clients cost?"

A cost report is the great-granddaddy of reports. Useful, cost-driven business metrics are the key to determining whether a marketing effort is an investment or a cost, and it is amazingly easy to do. These last two data points also are completed outside the Google Analytics framework because they include third-party cost data (which with some channels, such as Google Ads, can be brought into Google Analytics; by and large, this requires manual input into a simple Excel worksheet). With a well-configured Google Analytics account, *which includes accurate conversion tracking*, identifying which marketing channels drive conversions is a tedious, albeit achievable, prospect.

The final two business-based steps are to marry cost data to conversions, and ideally newly signed clients. Metrics for both should be reviewed monthly, or at a minimum, quarterly, and right before a business review or contract renewal with a vendor. Generating cost-per-inquiry data requires nothing more than a sophisticated tracking infrastructure and simple division: just divide the cost spent on that marketing channel by the number of conversions from that channel according to Google Analytics.

Even more valuable, and admittedly much more difficult, is determining cost-per-client—the final step before return on investment (ROI). Cost-per-client is the gold standard of business reporting for law firms, and very few firms get there. This is due, in no small part, to two different systems—marketing reporting infrastructure and case management—that aren't integrated. Ultimately, matching new matters opened in case management software to business reporting requires finding a common match among name, a phone number, or email address, and then going through the process, either manual or automated, of trying to tie that common element together, and then allocate marketing channels specifically to that new client. When this is done, to derive cost-per-client, simply divide the number of clients in each channel by the cost of that marketing channel. The extreme difficulty lies in matching that common element between the two different systems. There are a variety of tools—Law Ruler, Lexicata (recently purchased by Clio), Lawmatics, Captora, Avvo Ignite[26]—that have tried to automate this; however, none have really been effective because the internal systems in each law firm are either customized, unique, or nonexistent.[27] Software is simply a tool; it does not change the internal processes of the firm.

One Client, and It Will Pay for Itself!

There is no shortage of marketing channels on which lawyers can spend their money, and no shortage of advertising salespeople cold-calling lawyers to try to secure their money. One of the final, "Hail Mary" attempts that advertising salespeople employ to close the deal is the simple "*one client, and it will pay for itself*" pitch. This is especially easy to push in the legal industry, in which any individual client may in fact have a very high payout. However, "*one client, and it will pay for itself*" is completely misleading. A better way to interpret this is, "*if you only get one client, you are working for the advertiser.*" Marketing is an investment, and if you only make back the money you spent on an investment, the ROI is . . . 0.0%. Would you invest in a stock like this? Of course not. So, why would you invest in a marketing plan that had the same premise? A sales pitch premised on "*one client, and it will pay for itself*" indicates a salesman who either doesn't understand or who doesn't care about your business. He's either dumb or desperate to fill a quota.

---

26.   Note that Avvo's Ignite product has not been supported from a technology perspective for many years now.

27.   Clio's recent acquisition of Lexicata and subsequent rebranding to Clio Grow is the first true integration between marketing reporting and case management. It will be interesting to watch.

2

SEO: ORGANIC SEARCH

Organic Search refers to the not-for-pay, unmapped results that show up after a search query. Historically, these results showed up directly below the search query and were the primary focus of early SEO efforts. In fact, the acronym "SEO" is frequently (and incorrectly) used interchangeably with "Local SEO"—the mapped results that now show above the organic results for high-value terms like "personal injury lawyer New Orleans." I specify "incorrectly" because, with a few exceptions, the tactical elements that go into results in organic SEO are fundamentally different those that drive Local SEO.

Bill Gurley, the renowned venture capitalist, told me at an early Avvo board meeting that "SEO is free beer." It was this race toward free beer— free marketing, free traffic, free business—that came to define Avvo's marketing's tactical focus during the early years. Avvo's mastery of SEO was the primary factor that enabled a small, lean tech startup to leapfrog enormous, established competitors in the market—most notably FindLaw and Martindale-Hubbell. Of course, nothing is really free. Avvo's true cost was a small staff devoted to understanding the ever-changing vagaries of SEO. But the historical reference goes to show just how rapidly legal SEO has gone from unknown to a dominant marketing channel. In the 2006 to 2009 period, the entire SEO "team" at Avvo consisted of myself, consultant Alex Bennert, and a small group of developers who begrudgingly allocated time to SEO. The global field of SEO that was focused exclusively on the legal industry amounted to just a small handful of resources.[1] SEO tactics were rudimentary compared to the technical sophistication of today. Even the pace and extent of algorithmic changes was choppy and blunt, with large swings in performance meted out 1 to 3 times a year. This is especially true compared to today's much more fluid and consistent environment, in which the algorithms are constantly evolving and sites rarely see massive swings in performance.

Over the past 15 years, the legal industry has jumped aggressively into the SEO game, with countless agencies, consultants, in-house teams, and DIYers all entering the race for free beer. Which is why you find yourself reading this book.

The most important consideration to note is that Google's restructuring of the SERP has heavily shifted traffic away from Organic Search to Google Ads and Local Search results. Simply put, organic results frequently show only below the fold (i.e., the user must scroll to see them), after paid and Local Search results have been displayed. Despite that, we continue to see many firms generating a large volume of traffic (and, therefore, business) from Organic Search.

It's impossible to gain success in Organic Search without an understanding of the fundamentals of how it works. What follows is a high-level overview that explains how computers find, read, and rank content on the web.

---

1.   Useless historical footnote and personal musings: In all fairness, at this time (late 2006), my personal knowledge of SEO was extremely limited. I recall prepping for my interview at Avvo over beers with my MBA friend Mark Eamer, who at the time was running SEO for the budding real estate site Zillow. (Rich Barton, who formerly had started Expedia and was one of the earliest Avvo investors, founded Zillow. Avvo founder Mark Britton was Rich's General Counsel and right-hand man at Expedia.) Once at Avvo, I spent a lot of time learning the art and science from the small cadre of people who made up the SEO universe back then. It was a different world, a tight-knit, egalitarian community who openly shared information and was comprised of young, quirky, entrepreneurial technonerds who gathered both online and at Search Marketing eXpo (SMX) conferences fueled by Red Bull and vodka. Many people in the community of self-taught SEO experts had made and lost small fortunes in the three Ps: online porn, pills, and/or poker—markets that were highly profitable and almost completely unregulated (at the time). The group was heavily Canadian, but both old and young, and contrary to conventional wisdom, comprised of both men and women: Matt Siltala, Vanessa Fox, Ian Lurie, Rand Fishkin, Alex Bennert, Marshall Simmonds, Rhea Drysdale, Michael Gray, Todd Friesen, Lisa Baron, David Mihm, Matt McGee, Danny Dover, Duane Forrester, Danny Sullivan, and of course, Google's Matt Cutts (who was the only calculated, measured information-sharer). Fortunately for me, they were geographically concentrated not in Silicon Valley but in the Pacific Northwest.

Finding Content: Crawling

How do search engines become aware of webpages and websites? It's a simple question with a somewhat complex answer. Search engines use programs that follow links from one webpage to another; they discover and catalogue new pages as they follow those links. Each page that has more links provides the search engine with more pages (and websites) to discover. These programs frequently are referred to as "bots," "spiders," or "crawlers." The process of moving through these links and discovering new webpages and websites is called crawling. Google's bot is called Googlebot, and Bing's bot is . . . Bingbot. (Yahoo was much more creative and called its bot Slurp.) The key here is that without a link pointing to a piece of content, the search engines will remain blissfully unaware that that content even exists. The contrapositive states that content that has many different pages linking to it will be found extremely quickly. Thus, one of the key elements in publishing new content is ensuring that there are links pointing to it, so Google can find it. This is especially important for time-sensitive content—traditionally, news publishers. In the legal world, this frequently is less of an issue, although some extremely responsive and aggressive personal injury lawyers may publish content immediately after a large accident in an attempt to generate business, recall the duck boat accidents in Seattle and Florida, for example. In a more extreme time-sensitive example, my team pre-empted the VW emissions scandal prepping content prior to the breaking of the story. Getting that content crawled as quickly as possible (i.e., before competitors' content is crawled) becomes an important tactical element of success.

One of the huge limitations of search engine bots is that all they can really do is follow links to more content. Clearly, they can't type. This means that the search engines most likely can't find content that can only be accessed by typing. The obvious example here is content contained on sites that require a password. Think of all the Facebook content, for example. This huge treasure trove of password-protected content simply can't be accessed by a bot. Other examples include content that's contained in password-accessible news sites, or attorney profiles that can be accessed only via search queries on outdated state bar association sites.

Search engines don't necessarily crawl every single page on a website. The number of pages a bot will crawl on any given website is determined by the crawl budget for a site. Bots favor sites with a strong backlink profile and unique, high-quality content. Bots use those elements to find lots of interesting pages on highly authoritative sites. The reverse is also true—low-authority sites that are primarily populated with content that is thin, poorly written, or pilfered from other sites will find few of their pages crawled. This means that the search engines may never see the rare example of great content on a low-quality site—they simply aren't going to waste their crawl budget looking for it. Note that there is no published measure of a "crawl budget"—it's not a metric that Google publishes. Instead, crawl budget can be determined by viewing how many pages of content are on a site, and then assessing which of those pages have been crawled.

Understanding Crawl Budget with the Avvo Example

We can use the Avvo example to explain how to balance crawl budget and content volume. When Avvo launched, the potential number of webpages was extremely large due to the vast amount of data Avvo had collected, which included hundreds of thousands of lawyer profiles. The profiles could be cut and organized by practice area, as well as by a multiplicity of geographic slices—city, state, region, zip code, etc. Each of these "slices" could function as a new page. With the data we had, the site ostensibly could have been launched with 12 to 20 million different pages of content—all optimized for search results. However, as a brand-new website, Avvo literally had no domain authority (i.e., backlinks), and much of the content was extremely thin and generic. Avvo had to focus its search engine crawl budgets on a small set of pages—specifically, on high-value pages that *did* have unique content. Avvo further cut its potential page count by launching in only six states. Over time, as more and more profiles were filled out (generating more and more rich, interesting, and unique content) and more and more third-party sites linked to the domain (improving the site's authority), Avvo's crawl budget expanded. A larger crawl budget enabled Avvo to add more and more profile pages, expand into different states, and cut practice area lists by increasingly finite geographic boundaries (personal injury lawyer + city; personal injury lawyer + Zip code; personal injury lawyer + neighborhood, and so on). Yelp is a great example of a site that has used extremely high domain authority to generate a vast amount of high-value pages. Yelp has sliced and diced its directory into increasingly finite areas: pizza restaurants in Seattle, pizza restaurants in downtown Seattle, and even pizza restaurants near the Space Needle (no "Seattle" needed).

Search engines try to ensure that they don't miss any webpages by independently crawling every different URL. This means that what may look like the same page to humans is actually multiple pages to a bot. For example, the following URLs all contain identical content about pink, fuzzy, bunny slippers. But because the URLs are different, the bot must crawl each of them independently, in the off chance that the content is different:

http://fuzzybunnyslippers.com/pink
https://fuzzybunnyslippers.com/pink
http://www.fuzzybunnyslippers.com/pink
https://www.fuzzybunnyslippers.com/pink
https://FuzzyBunnySlippers.com/pink
https://www.FuzzyBunnySlippers.com/pink
https://fuzzybunnyslippers.com/pink.html
https://fuzzybunnyslippers.com/pink/
https://fuzzybunnyslippers.com/pink?size=10
https://fuzzybunnyslippers.com/pink?ads-Facebook

Common examples of duplicating pages on a website include having both secure (http) and nonsecure (https) sites; www and non-www versions; case-sensitive URL text; and parameterized URLs. Parameters in a URL are followed by the question mark (?) in the preceding example. In the example, parameterized URLs are distinct URLs that display pink fuzzy bunny slippers in size 10 or track advertising from a Facebook campaign. Some website platforms that weren't designed with SEO in mind frequently include other elements in a URL. Common examples are appending.html to the end of a URL or adding an unnecessary trailing slash "/" at the end.

A poorly designed content management system (CMS) that inadvertently generates multiple, different versions of a URL, all of which represent the same content (or extremely similar—think different pages for different shoe sizes, for example) is a serious problem in light of a crawl budget. Unintentionally duplicated pages can have a very significant negative effect on search performance as search engines exhaust their crawl budget sifting through page after page of identical content. Imagine if all the pages in this book were identical. Someone flipping through would quickly return the book to the shelf in favor of something more interesting. To stretch the analogy even further, it would be a long time before the user came back to the book, just like search engines that return much less frequently to sites that look like a book that has identical pages.

Considering Content: Indexing

Just because Google has crawled (i.e., found) content doesn't necessarily mean that that content is now in the consideration set for search results (i.e., something that Google might show to a searcher). To show up in search results, webpages need to be not only found, but also indexed. Search engines decide to index content on a wide variety of factors, which ultimately can be boiled down to, "*Is this the original version of well-written, interesting content?*" For example, in the case of our unintentionally duplicated pages, Google may crawl hundreds of versions of URLs of the same content, yet index only one of those pages. This ensures that Google won't show multiple pages of identical content from the same site to a single searcher (which would be a horrendously poor user experience).

You can see the set of webpages on a website that are indexed by doing a search on Google. Simply enter **site:<example.com>** to see all of the content indexed on your domain. This is one of the first things I do when reviewing a site, because the results can be extremely revealing on two levels. First, the results show the sheer volume of pages indexed by Google. This gives a hint of the overall authority of the site (lots of indexed pages indicate a more authoritative site), as well as the firm's overall content strategy (have they been pushing four blog posts a week for the past three years, or is the site a bare-bones, eight-page site that serves as little more than an inadequate online placeholder). Second, and more interestingly, the **site:** search may expediently reveal significant problems with the site's overall technical platform. All website owners should periodically run a **site:** search to see whether their understanding of the content on their site is the same as Google's. Another approach to researching indexed content on a site is to download the list directly from Google Search Console. Some common things to look for:

- **Porn, pirated movies, and dating pages**—Among other things that a **site:** search can uncover is content published on the domain as the result of being hacked. I've sat in more than a few lawyer meetings in which we've uncovered downloadable porn, pirated copies of *When Harry Met Sally*, and more dating pages than I care to remember.
- **HTTP versus HTTPS**—By now, many sites have transitioned to the secure version of a website (https) instead of continuing to use the standard, nonsecure version (http) of a website. A poorly executed

conversion may affect some pages on a site, but not all. Perusing the results in the **site:** search may reveal pages that are still nonsecure (just look for *http* instead of *https*).

- **www versus non-www**—Many sites use the www version of URLs, while others drop the www (which technically is a subdomain). There is no inherent advantage to using one or the other. Many website CMSs unintentionally create pages in both versions (for example, www.mypages.com and mypages.com). Having two versions on a site is a problem because it creates duplicate content and it causes the spider to crawl twice as many pages as necessary. This, as you know by now, exhausts the crawl budget without returning an advantage. This problem is especially common among sites that have received a site "upgrade" or redesign. The new developer launches a non-www version, ignoring the fact that the site was originally built on www, and leaves the "old" content in place beside the new. In many cases, the entire site is duplicated verbatim with both versions.

- **Garbage pages**—"Garbage page" isn't technically an SEO term, but a catchall for random files and other assorted pages that are useless to the user. Open each page. If the page looks like it may not be useful to a user, it probably shouldn't be indexed.

- **WordPress sample pages**—Unsophisticated website designers frequently design and then craft a WordPress site from preexisting WordPress themes. Themes essentially are a starter design template. These themes almost always contain example pages, and designers with limited development skills frequently launch the site with some of those example pages. This is a common error seen on WordPress sites that are built by well-intentioned DIYers. While the sample pages may seem entirely hidden, Google most likely can find them. You can verify that by running a **site:** search. (The most widespread unintentional WordPress sample page is called "Hello World.")

Another tool you can use to check on what content Google has indexed on a site is Google Search Console. Search Console graphically displays three months of indexed content. Dramatic changes in this index count can indicate technical concerns. For example, a large, sudden upswing in indexed pages may indicate pages that have been unintentionally created. Search Console previously stored only 90 days of data, but recently expanded to store 16 months of data. The data is now available via API. To truly store Search Console index count data, it is best to download and store the API file.

The following stacked area graph depicts the fundamental differences in how pages are treated as reflected in the different number of pages in the these categories: sitemap, crawl, index, and entry pages.[2]

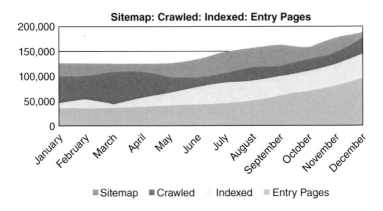

Not all pages on a website should be indexed; in fact, many shouldn't. There are simply some pages that offer zero value to someone searching Google. For example, a "thank you" page that shows up after someone signs up for a newsletter or the login page to the site's CMS system. These pages can be "no-indexed"—a command that essentially tells Google to not index the page should the bots find it. No-indexing is a great strategy for handling website content that has been copied verbatim from elsewhere on the Internet. No-indexing this content ensures that Google doesn't penalize a site for copying the content. Content that exists elsewhere on the web is common on law firm websites. For example, we have a client who catalogues specific laws, state by state, for a very niche legal practice. This content is extremely helpful to the site's users; however, because it is literally verbatim cut-and-pasted from various state government sites, we need to ensure that Google doesn't think the site is simply cribbing content from

---

2.   I wrote about these flavors of page categories in 2011: Conrad Saam, *How to Terrify Executives into Linkbuilding* SEARCH ENGINE LAND (Nov. 16, 2011), https://searchengineland .com/terrify_executives_linkbuildin-101065. Things haven't really changed much at all since then.

across the web. We handle this by no-indexing the pages on which that content resides.

Be extremely careful when discouraging Google from skipping content on a website; it is fairly easy to inadvertently no-index much more content that you had intended. In other words, "Don't try this at home, kids." In the following example, the Minnesota State Bar tells Google not to crawl its entire site by the way its Robots.txt file is written. Note **disallow: /**, which instructs Google to *not* crawl any URLs beyond the first /. (The organization has since fixed this.)

Canonical Tags

One of the tools Google implemented to help website owners manage all these potential variants of URLs is the use of canonical tags. *Canonical* comes from the word *canon*—or "the original." Thus, canonical tags can be used to define the original version of a webpage. More concretely, you can define the canonical version of the page http://www.example.com/ConradIsAwesome/ with a canonical tag that defines the original version as https://example.com /conradisawesome. The canonical tag ensures that only the defined canonical version of the page is indexed. While this may seem like a reasonably elegant way of handling an unsophisticated CMS system, note that this is really just a band-aid. First, the canonical tags don't reduce the number of pages being crawled. Google still has to crawl the page to even find the canonical tag. Second, canonical tags frequently are implemented incorrectly or are outdated. This is especially true in a large-scale "upgrade" to a website. For example, we've seen many sites upgrade from http to https, but not upgrade the canonical tags—the new https version of a page now marks the legacy http version as the canonical version, which undercuts all the value of the https upgrade. In general, it is best to use a sophisticated, current CMS system to avoid unintentionally duplicating pages instead of relying on the canonical tag band-aid.

Sitemaps

One of the early tools created to help search engines find and index all this important content was the sitemap. A sitemap essentially is a map of all the content on a website. There are two versions of a sitemap—the first is the HTML (or on-site) sitemap. An HTML sitemap essentially is a series of links that drives bots to all the pages on a website. Naturally, this gets somewhat cumbersome for even moderately large sites. The second version is an XML[3] sitemap. An XML sitemap essentially is a published XML data feed that's seen only by search engines, and which lists all the pages on the website. Google enabled webmasters to prioritize the importance of different pages on a website by applying a 1 to 10 scale of priority on each page. A nice idea, but the overriding consensus among SEO agencies is that these priority scores have nothing to do with SEO performance.

XML sitemaps typically are dynamically generated by sophisticated content management systems. They're updated when new content is added to the website. Because XML sitemaps are automatically generated, a common concern is the existence of multiple conflicting sitemaps for the same website. Consider getting two maps for Baltimore, one from 1968 and one from yesterday. But you're a dumb computer and can't determine which one is which, or which one is more recent and which is outdated. Dated legacy sitemaps are a frequent problem with sites that have been "upgraded" by designers or developers who have limited SEO expertise. (The theme of "upgraded" websites being the cause of problems is very common. If you've ever redesigned or "upgraded" your website, especially if you've changed CMSs, it's best to assume that the implementation has been poorly executed vis-à-vis SEO technical best practices.)

Reading Content (How Does a Computer Know What a Webpage Is About?)

So, now that Google can find content, how does a computer understand what a webpage is about? Is this a page about the best microbrews in Denver or a retail page selling pink fuzzy bunny slippers, or the web's most insightful page about truck accident lawyers in Atlanta? The foundational answer is surprisingly rudimentary: the bots simply count and catalogue words on a page. Simply put, a page with a high word count for the word *beer* probably is about . . . beer. Google has significantly improved its ability to semantically understand what content is about vis-à-vis human language.

---

3.   An Extensible Markup Language (XML) file can be described as a text file that is human- and machine-readable through defined markup.

Essentially, the combination of words, phrases, and context are all deciphered (to some extent) to understand a page's content. Thus, computers can differentiate between a page about great beer, a page about the history of beer, a page about where to buy beer, and a page that contains Conrad's list of his favorite IPA beers. Now, it's not that flagrantly simplistic. A page that has no words other than the content *beer beer beer beer beer beer beer beer beer beer beer beer beer beer beer beer beer beer beer* isn't going to really be about beer. (Hint: It's likely that *beer* is camouflage.)[4]

Not all words on a page have the same weight as they pertain to helping search engines understand what a page is about. Put simply, some words are more important than others, and those words are called out specifically by code on the website. This occasionally is referred to as on-page or on-site SEO.

Title Tag

The title tag of a page is what it sounds like—the title of the page. While this content never visually shows up on the page itself, it does show up as the link in the SERPs that users click to get to the content. Thus, the title tag is extremely important. Note that there is a limited character count for what search engines will show for that link, so very long title tags get snipped. Title tags that exceed the character limit end with a series of dots: . . .. The current character limit for a title tag on Google and Bing is 50 to 60 characters.[5] Keeping title tags below the 60-character count displays the title as intended more than 90% of the time.[6] Not surprisingly, search engines put very heavy weight on the words inside a title tag when determining what a page is about.

A major problem with title tags on the WordPress platform is generated by the widely used (and somewhat helpful) SEO plug-in, Yoast. In an attempt to make SEO easier and more automated, there are settings in Yoast that are

---

4. One of the old-school SEO black-hat tactics was to load up a page with hidden, repetitive keywords to manipulate their understanding of what a page was about. Staying with our beer example, consider a webpage that has a white background with the word "beer" repeated ad nauseum and styled in white font on that white background. The user would never "see" the repetitive, spammy, unnatural content, yet a computer could be easily fooled into changing its perspective of what that webpage was really about. Don't try this at home kids . . . the search engines caught onto this decades ago.

5. The limit actually is pixels. 600 right now in Google. And Google has been known to extend that for some SERPs. So consider these length "guidelines" instead of firm limits.

6. According to a study by Moz. Read more at https://moz.com/learn/seo/title-tag.

designed to automatically append content (frequently, the company name or brand) to the end of each title tag—often separated from the defined title tag by the "|" symbol. In some poor implementations of Yoast on Word-Press, the title tag is not defined and instead, each page is "appended" with the value entered in the Company Name field. This means that every single page has the exact same title. Imagine walking into a library where all of the books had the same title.

In general, well-known brands have some advantage in generating more clicks. Adding a brand to the title tag may make sense to increase conversions. However, in the legal world, consumers are much less brand-aware and loyal to brands than, say, in the automotive space. People simply can't name lawyers, nor do they have a specific affinity for one law firm over another. Furthermore, many law firms have ridiculously long, partner-centric brand names—Stanley, Britton, Tsakalakis, King, Ramsey, and Saam, L.L.P., for example. Appending these long—and essentially meaningless, to the prospect—names to the end of a title tag has two negative results. First, they will almost always get chopped off, leaving the displayed title tag ending in "Motorcycle Accident Attorney | Stanley, Britton, Tsak. . . ." Second, they dilute the meaningful content in the title tag. This is no longer a page about "motorcycle accident attorney," but instead, a page about "Motorcycle Accident Attorney | Stanley, Britton, Tsakalakis, King, Ramsey, and Saam, L.L.P." And Google has no idea what a Britton is (*someone from England?*), nor how a Tsakalakis is related to the practice of motorcycle accident litigation, nor who King Ramsey is (*did he ride a motorcycle?*). In the unbranded universe of legal, including the firm name in the title tag dilutes the focus of the content, especially for long name-branded firms.

H1 and H2 Tags

Words contained in the H1 tag are expressly important in defining (to a search engine) what a webpage is about. The H1 tag is HTML code that defines the primary heading (H1) of a webpage. H1 tags initially were used in Cascading Style Sheets (CSS) to specify font size and style for important content. The very simple theory is this: H1 tags are used to specify the most visually prominent content—think boldfaced and large-sized font. Search engines use content literally highlighted with that visual prominence (as defined by the H1 code) as being extra heavily weighted for defining the overall content of the page vis-à-vis the content on that page. Note that each page should have one and only one H1 tag, because it denotes the primary heading for the page. Frequently, the title tag and the H1 are identical.

CSS also specifies a series of heading tags that have lesser visual emphasis—H2, H3, etc. This code, often call "H tags," is used to visually denote (via font size and style) subheadings of content—again, to help a search engine understand what a page is about.[7]

The H tags all seem fairly straightforward. However, developers and designers not well-versed in SEO principles frequently misuse them. Developers can use CSS to specify the font, style, and size of H tags. This flexibility means that, frequently, lazy or uninformed developers utilize H tags to their own purposes, and not necessarily to call out important heading content of a page. We frequently see H1s casually used in templates for foundational content. For example, a developer may visually highlight the "Contact Us" content that shows up in a template by using the H1 tag. Because that content shows up in the template, this means that every single page on the site has a primary heading of . . . "Contact Us." For a computer that reads code to understand what a page is about, this is not just useless but proactively harmful, because now, every single page has the same H1. Consider if this book's chapters were all titled "Contact Us."

Many pages end up accidentally having multiple H1s—another SEO no-no, in that there can only be one primary heading about a specific piece of content.[8] This is particularly common with poorly coded WordPress themes that have H1s inappropriately incorporated into the theme. Note that with most WordPress themes, the H1 is automatically defined as the title of the page. This seems logical; however, a well-intentioned writer also can select an H1 tag (or multiple H1 tags) when adding content. So, she can inadvertently generate multiple H1 tags.[9] A simple best practice is to not utilize WordPress to define an H1, but instead use the H2s as subheadings.

---

7.   For SEO purposes, the emphasis for H tags is placed heavily on the H1. Recent comments from Duane Forrester, formerly of Bing, suggest that Bing and Google both looked only up to the first H2 to help define page content. Suffice to say, it is extremely important that the H1 tag be representative of the overall content of the page.

8.   Multiple H2s are fine. H2s are considered subheadings and, therefore, they denote unique pieces of content on a page.

9.   I've often wondered why there isn't a WordPress plug-in to disable authors from specifying H1 tags. This would essentially idiot-proof the CMS from this problem.

Meta Description

Another piece of content associated with a page but also unseen by users is the meta description. This is a set of short sentences that summarize what the page is about. The meta description shows up on the SERPs, directly below a site's the clickable title tag. Meta descriptions are best thought of as your opportunity to compete for the user's click among the other 9 Organic Search results. Note that just like title tags, meta descriptions have a character limit. In mid-May 2018, displayed meta descriptions reverted to their former count of roughly 155 to 160 characters. Historically, for pages that lack meta descriptions, Google would guesstimate a summary and select a small snippet of content in lieu of a missing meta description. Over the past three years, Google has increasingly overruled displaying a defined meta description in favor of its own estimation of the summary of that page (much to the annoyance of SEO agencies everywhere). Additionally, meta descriptions have become decreasingly important and are not considered a ranking factor. There are many different strategies that could be successful for meta descriptions now. Leaving them out completely for Google to pull whatever Google is going to pull from the content that's most relevant to the query is one. Having an optimized description and still understanding that Google will pull whatever it thinks is best is another. Suffice to say, this is not a tactic to obsess over.

Meta Keywords

Meta Keywords are another relic that unfortunately haven't gone the way of the dinosaur yet.[10] Dating to the extremely early days of SEO, meta keywords were a way of defining what a page was about. At that point in the history of SEO, search engines were neophytes in their semantic sophistication. Thus, queries for "car accident attorney" and an "auto wreck law firm" were considerably more semantically different than they are today. The practice of "tagging" content with meta keywords was an attempt to tell Google what the content was about, and also to capture verbal variations. The ensuing lists of meta keywords (which invariably leveraged all variants of "lawyer," "attorney," and "law firm") with which any given page was tagged provides either hilarity or tedium, depending on your mood: *car accident lawyer, car accident attorney, auto accident lawyer, auto accident attorney, car accident law firm, auto accident law firm, car accident*

---

10.   Read more at https://webmasters.googleblog.com/2009/09/google-does-not-use -keywords-meta-tag.html.

lawyers, car accident attorneys, car wreck lawyer, car wreck attorney, car crash lawyer, car wreck attorney. . . .

Fortunately, Google very publicly put a stop to all uses of meta keywords. However, many people never got the message, and well-meaning SEO agencies diligently continued to "tag" content with an increasingly ludicrous series of synonyms. At this point, a page that is tagged with meta tags is an indication of either an extremely dated site or an SEO specialist who has no idea what he is doing. Smart firms should immediately fire any SEO specialist or agency that talks about the importance of meta tags. Legacy tags don't really do any harm other than take up a very small amount of file size. From a best-practices perspective, we typically delete existing meta tags, although this falls into a very low priority.

The emphasis on "tagging" content within the underinformed SEO community led to an extremely common and significant problem with WordPress sites. In WordPress, authors can tag their content to define what it is about. These WordPress tags are not to be confused with meta tags (although they frequently are). Functionally, a WordPress tag generates a new page of content that's optimized for that content and that tag, which includes a small snippet of the content from that page and all other pages with the same tag. These pages typically are published here: mywebsite.com/tag/example.[11]

The problem, of course, is that these pages are extremely thin—just a short snippet of content that already exists on the same website. This becomes exponentially worse if the historical approach to meta tags is erroneously implemented through these WordPress tags. Remember the tactic of diligently using meta keywords to try to capture every variation of "car wreck attorney"? Each of those variations applied to the WordPress tags will generate yet another page—with nothing more than a simple snippet of content that's duplicated across each and every page. We've seen sites with thousands of these thin pages, all taking up crawl budget, all with extremely thin content, and all demonstrating to the search engines that the overall content mix of that particular site is extremely low-quality. In general (and with occasional exceptions), these tag pages do nothing to generate inbound SEO traffic; a generic rule of thumb recommends not using them at all. For legacy problems—that is, how to handle these pages once they exist—we recommend deleting or

---

11. In fact, you can use a site: search to determine whether your site has many of these pages generated by WordPress tags. Simply try **site:<mywebsite.com>/tag/** to see all of the pages on your website that were created by WordPress tags. (Note that this assumes that the site structure is built out as described in this chapter.)

no-indexing these WordPress pages, so they don't reflect poorly on the overall site. Your efforts to delete or no-index these tagged pages in WordPress will decrease the overall page count, increase the concentration of high-quality content on the website, and actually result in increased SEO traffic.[12]

Confusing, isn't it? It's easy to understand how underinformed SEO agencies and well-meaning DIYers accidentally embraced these WordPress tags, thinking they were "tagging" their content with meta keywords. In turn, they sabotaged their own site's performance by unintentionally creating hundreds or even thousands of pages that no human reader would find interesting.

But deleting these pages has performance implications. The following graphs show an increase in website traffic (top graph) coinciding with a decrease in page count (bottom graph):

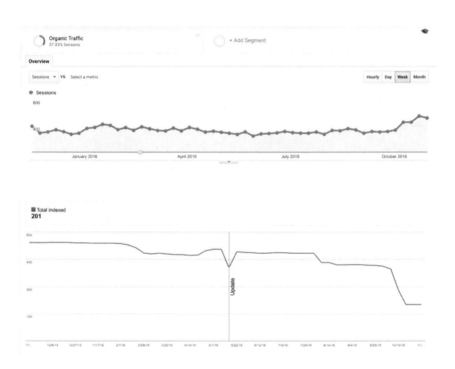

---

12.   I published a series of articles in Search Engine Land to showcase lawyer websites that the agency deliberately reduced page count for, maximizing the crawl budget and improving the concentration of quality content. The net result was that traffic increased as page count decreased—which runs contrary to the oft-touted strategy of "content is king." You can see the details at Conrad Saam, *More Content, Less Traffic: Part I*, SEARCH ENGINE LAND (Dec. 7, 2016), https://searchengineland.com/content-less-traffic-part-262960, and Conrad Saam, *More Content, Less Traffic: Part II*, SEARCH ENGINE LAND (Jul. 3, 2017), https://searchengineland.com/content-less-traffic-part-ii-277374.

Multilingual Content

As discussed ad nauseum, SEO is viciously competitive in the legal industry. An under-competitive channel a law firm can leverage is multilingual websites. When properly configured, multilingual sites have an unfair advantage in both Organic Search and Paid Search. Essentially, there are few other websites that offer "car accident lawyer" in Spanish, or Polish, or Hindi. And although the volume may be very low, a well-configured site can capture close to 100% of that market if there are no competitors.

Running multilingual sites takes much more than simply putting up a page that says, "hablo español" (that tack simply tries to make a site rank for the keyword "hablo español"). The next level of poorly implemented multilingual is content that's simply translated (and note that the translations should be done by a human instead of a computer; computers simply can't capture the nuances of language and make it read correctly). These translated pages often are stuck onto an existing English-based template, with navigation, etc., all in a different language—far from a fully immersive experience. It is typically very easy to assess whether the technology behind the multilingual site is poorly configured by searching the code for the term "lang." Frequently, we see Spanish content that has a **lang=en** marker, which essentially defines the language of the page as being in English. Done correctly, the underlying code for a multilingual site does two things: 1) provides a fully immersive experience, so the user experiences the entire site in her language (meaning everything—navigation, buttons, etc.), and 2) defines to the search engines which pages are the same, just in different languages—i.e., this car accident page in French is that same as this one in English. The implementation of this code frankly is technical, tricky, and best left to a high-quality agency. Running two sites in two different languages is a worst practice. To the best of my knowledge, none of the legally focused proprietary platforms provide efficient multilingual code support—another reason to rely on WordPress-based websites.

Organic Search Element: Authority

Google was not the first search engine, nor the second or the third or even the fifteenth. Those of you from my generation will recall cereal boxes ubiquitously stuffed with CDs to install American Online.[13] Remember dogpile,

---

13. Fair or not, nothing shouts, "I'm a relic and I'm not up with technology" than an AOL email address, a Yahoo address, and, increasingly, a Gmail address, which look personal instead of professional. All lawyers should communicate via email with an email address from their own domain. It's simply more professional and easily implemented through Google's Gmail system.

AskJeeves (which became Ask.com), Excite, AltaVista, Webcrawler, Lycos, or Netscape's Infoseek? Google leapfrogged all of these competitors because it was the first to utilize links from other websites as a proxy of the quality of content to which those links were pointing. This is the foundation of website authority, and this was revolutionary because it enabled Google to generate search results that were radically superior to all other search engines. The basic premise is very simple: authors will link to other webpages to share great content with their own readers, and those links are a proxy for the quality of the linked content. Also note that authority is one of the few tactical elements that affects both Organic Search and Local Search. And, it's a primary differentiator for both; it drives performance in very competitive markets like legal.

The Relative Importance of This Section

As discussed many times earlier, the online legal marketplace is extremely competitive. All the other chapters in this book discuss tactics, techniques, and technologies that are frankly table stakes for success—without them, most law firms simply can't compete online. Authority (links to a site) is the primary differentiator that separates the wheat from the chaff in the online battle for clients. One of the unfortunate results of this is that brand-new firms find it very difficult to compete. A decade ago, when very few lawyers understood even the basic fundamentals of SEO, the web was a great level setter. Small firms led by nerdy, tech-leaning lawyers aggressively grew their firms under the noses of slower, stodgy, conservative incumbents. Those days are long dead, and small and newly formed firms are at a distinct disadvantage now when competing online. This is primarily due to the cost, time, and difficulty involved in generating backlinks to a domain. When firms split up, as they often do, the fight over ownership of the domain can and should be a very contentious negotiation. I have found myself on more than one occasion caught between former partners sparring over ownership of the legacy domain, essentially fighting over the backlink profile that can be the difference between a successful new firm launch and a resounding belly flop.

Backlink Nuances: Authority

A website that has a lot of links pointing to it holds a lot of authority—the many links from many different sources indicate a website that has content of very high quality. What logically follows is that links from websites that have high authority are more valuable than links from websites that have low authority. In practice, this is very simple to understand: a link to a law firm website from the *New York Times* (which has a huge volume of links pointing to it) is much more valuable than a link from www.Conrads DonutShop.com. High-value links translate into better performance in search queries. Essentially, good content about motorcycle accidents will perform better (rank higher and drive more traffic) if it lives on a highly authoritative domain than on a domain that has zero links. In addition, links from local websites (for example, the local Chamber of Commerce) carry much greater weight in helping sites rank for local queries.

Authority also is determined at the page level. In general, a link on a page that is closer to the homepage (in terms of clicks away from the homepage) are much more valuable than a link on a page that's buried deep in a website. Using our *New York Times* example, a link on www.nyt.com to a law firm website lends much more authority to that website than, say, a link from www.nyt.com/archives/september/2004/article8. A further nuance is that webpages that have many external or internal (from within the same domain) links pointing to them tend to have more authority than pages devoid of links. Thus, in our www.nyt.com September 2004, Article 8 example, if that post had been particularly insightful or newsworthy and generated a lot of links back in 2004, the corresponding links coming from that Article 8 page would have correspondingly more authority than another page on the same domain that was devoid of links.

Internal links are links from within a site. Internal links also can be used to transfer some authority to a particular page. A link from the law firm's homepage to a lawyer's profile page can help that profile page rank well for the lawyer's name. You see this frequently with tangential topics on a law firm website linking to each other. The process of using internal links to improve Organic Search performance is called link sculpting.

Anchor Text

The anchor text of a link is the actual words in the link that can be clicked. For many years, the anchor text of a link was extremely beneficial in Organic Search performance. For example, a link that used the words "Best Seattle Divorce Lawyer" would help the target page for that link rank for variants of the search term "best Seattle divorce lawyer." This specific tactic was so overplayed and manipulated by SEO agencies, that on April 24, 2012, Google abruptly announced that not only was it no longer considering anchor text as a ranking factor, but Google would penalize sites that overdid the use of anchor text.[14] This "over-optimization" penalty caused a mass change in how link building was undertaken. For an example of the (historical) power of anchor text, consider the 2004 case of the search term "miserable failure." When this term was typed into the search engines, the results were pages for President George W. Bush. This was accomplished by a coordinated campaign among left-leaning SEO experts who used links with the anchor text "miserable failure" to point toward the White House bio page for George Bush. This gag is known as a Google Bomb and frequently targets politicians.[15]

Google's focus on links and the importance of backlink profiles in driving SEO success has inspired many studies and analyses to try to determine just which links have what impact. In an attempt to help SEO agencies understand and quantify a website's overall authority, three major tools have evolved that score a site's backlink profile. All three tools assess domain authority (the overall authority of a domain as a whole) on a nonlinear 0 to 100 scale.[16] This scale extends down to the page level (frequently called some variant of "page authority"). The first, and most widely used among newcomers to the SEO game, is the Link Explorer tool from Moz. This was one of the earliest tools created by Rand Fishkin; the tool was formerly known as Open Site Explorer.[17] In general, although there is much more

---

14.   I was in the audience at an SMX event when this was announced by then-Google SEO spokesman Matt Cutts. It caused immediate panic among SEO nerds in attendance, who hurriedly scurried back to their computers to undo all the anchor text they had dutifully been relying on for years.

15.   If you'd like to take this further, research the Google Bomb associated with Rick Santorum's homophobic comments and the SEO fallout orchestrated with anchor text–specific links by sex columnist Dan Savage. Fair warning: Suffice it to say that my ABA editors would have deleted that example from this manuscript.

16.   By nonlinear, I mean that a score of 20 is much more than twice as strong as a score of 10.

17.   In an unfortunate move, the flamboyant Fishkin was nudged/forced out of Moz. Following his departure, much if not all of the community team that built Moz as an SEO force was also unceremoniously let go. Love him or hate him, this was a large loss for the SEO community as a whole. Rand and the Moz SEO community did more than anyone else to reach and teach SEO newbies. Many of the best, well-maintained, and well-written resources for people beginning to understand online marketing were driven by Rand and the Moz community managers. The loss of Rand means that Moz now is nothing more than another suite of tools competing in a now grossly oversaturated market. And the Moz tools, frankly, have fallen behind newer, less well-known entrants.

free access from the Moz tool, we find Link Explorer to be less directionally useful than the other two tools that are available: Ahrefs and Majestic. At Mockingbird, we rely on Ahrefs. At the risk of grossly overgeneralizing, typically, we find well-performing sites in larger geographic markets along the following guidelines for domain rank:

Personal Injury: 45 to 65

Criminal Defense: 35 to 55

Family | Immigration | Estate Planning | Employment | Corporate | Bankruptcy: 20 to 40

In general, firms in smaller geographic markets (think Spokane versus Seattle) that have fewer firms with which to compete require a commensurately lower authority score. In some very small markets, or in a more obscure or specialized practice area, a basic backlink profile (getting a score to the low teens) may be all that's required for SEO success. Having quantified all of this, I can't stress enough that these scores are, at best, bad approximations of authority. Innumerable additional elements determine how a site will perform.

Note that the distribution of links across multiple domains is extremely important. In overly simplistic terms, 100 links from a single domain is much less valuable than 1 link from 100 different domains. Taken to its logical extreme, a domain that links to a website 1,000 or 10,000 times is much more an indication of programmatically generated spam links and is harmful. Typically, an at-a-glance evaluation of a backlink profile looks at the number of different high-value domains, not the sheer volume of links. An extremely blunt instrument to assess the quality of backlinks is to divide the total number of links by the total number of linking domains.

It's important to note that none of these third-party authority-measuring tools are extremely accurate, and scores across different tools frequently contradict each other. Yet, directionally, they are helpful guides. A 0 to 100 score is only helpful with context—scores are only relative against direct competitors. Also note that the tools measure authority on the web overall. As such, they fail at taking into account the unique value of local links to local companies (such as law firms). Consensus among advanced SEO agencies who focus on localized businesses is that localized links are key to SEO performance in Organic Search, and especially in Local Search. Backlink measurement tools fail to capture this reality. Simply put, a law firm in Atlanta that has a site with a domain rank of 20 may well outperform a competing firm's site that has a domain rank of 40 if the former's backlink profile is predominantly comprised of links from within the greater Atlanta market.

Not all links are helpful. In fact, some can proactively work against the success of an SEO campaign. The sheer value of links in driving success on Google meant that many SEOs tried to game the system by creating all sorts of different link schemes to fuel domain authority. This is known as link spam. Google has fought back against these various link schemes algorithmically (by using computers to identify these links) and manually (having humans walk through links by hand). The most well-known of these updates is the Penguin algorithm update that was officially launched in 2012. Penguin identified sites that were propped up by what Google deemed to be unnatural link profiles. Google actively punished those sites by reducing their presence in the SERPs. The resulting chaos and fluctuation in SEO performance was extreme. Since then, Google has taken a more gradual and less public approach to rolling out algorithmic changes as they pertain to link spam.

The primary categories of link spam are:

- **Link exchanges**—The simplest form of link spam, link exchanges are a mutual link backscratching—you link to mine and I'll link to yours. Obviously, link exchanges are extremely easy for Google to identify algorithmically.
- **Link networks**—A link network is simply a group of sites that all agree to link to each other. The linking can be done manually (i.e., an informal group of attorneys in different markets all agreeing to link to each other) or programmatically (i.e., an agency installing code across its client list to cross-link its websites).[18] In the legal marketspace, LexBlog used a blogroll (a list of links to other blogs) installed on all of its clients' blogs to drive link authority across its

---

18.   My very first consulting client, long before I established the agency, was a law firm on the Eastern seaboard that maintained its own link network of over 1,000 active domains— all registered to the same person. The partner contacted me after Google uncovered the firm's backlink scheme (which had heretofore been successful at driving authority), and the firm's website traffic cratered. Despite best efforts, the firm was never able to regain its former, link spam–driven success. This is one of many examples in which spammy tactics deliver great, albeit short-lived, results.

entire portfolio. This was extremely effective until Google caught on and the blogrolls had to be removed. This type of link network is called a Private Blog Network and was historically effective at link building due to the casual language, timely content, and ease of setting up blogs.

- **Link wheels**—A scheme in which website A links to website B which links to website C which links to website D . . . and eventually a link comes back in to website A. These were designed to be more difficult to algorithmically detect than simple link exchanges or link networks, although Google has become particularly adept at identifying links within link wheels.

- **Purchased links**—As backlinks became increasingly valuable in SEO performance, many website owners began monetizing their own domain authority by selling links. Typically, sites that have higher domain authority have commanded a commensurately higher price because they transferred more value. These links are obviously contrary to Google's SEO best practices—they do *not* convey any sense of the quality of the content, just the depth of the pockets of the link purchaser. Given the importance of links in Google's algorithm, the search engine behemoth has made a massive investment to combat paid links. Over time, as link building tactics have evolved, so has Google's sophistication—leading to a never-ending arms race between Google and spammy SEOs. Note that Google uses both algorithmic and manual (i.e., people) approaches to identify and penalize those who buy and sell links.

- **Low-authority, irrelevant domain links**—The importance of links prompted many in the early stages of the SEO industry to generate hundreds of thousands of links wherever they possibly could. This included websites that were stuffed with thousands of pages that listed different businesses but had only a link for "content." Other websites added pages that listed hundreds of links on a given page; these frequently were disguised as "directories." Many overseas sites started listing (and linking to) U.S. businesses. The web became littered with low-value content on low-value sites that linked to all sorts of businesses (along with optimized anchor text).

- **User-generated content and comment spam**—One of the easiest ways to build non-editorial links in the early days was to find websites that supported user-generated content and add content that included a link. The most widespread example of this was blog comments, where users could comment on a blog post. Comment spam is the practice of using linked blog comments (frequently with optimized anchor text) to drive SEO performance. Blog comments started to look farcical: "I thoroughly enjoyed your peanut soup recipe, thank you for sharing it with the community. I've found a touch of tarragon really brings out the smoky flavor while I am cooking in my <u>Best North Atlanta Car Wreck Lawyer Office</u>."

Google historically has combatted low-end links through penalties—essentially a drastic drop in Organic Search traffic when a site has been shown to manipulate links (either on the buyer or on the seller side). This happens both algorithmically and individually. One way that Google handles monitoring spammy links is through public reporting. Their online resource for reporting paid links can be found here: https://www.google .com/webmasters/tools/paidlinks.

Negative SEO Attack

Link-based penalties opened the door for an extremely nefarious, underhanded, and unethical practice of negative SEO attacks. In a negative SEO attack, a slew of bad links are purchased and pointed toward a competitor in hopes of instigating a Google penalty. More than a few law firms have engaged in this dirty practice, and the results can be financially devastating to their targets. One firm in the greater New York area successfully built their SEO strategy on negative SEO attacks. The firm successfully targeted a list of 15 to 20 competitors and pushed them entirely out of the SERPs. Responding to negative SEO attacks included the painstaking, time-consuming, and expensive process of disavowing links (telling Google which links to ignore) and then building up a stronger link profile. The following graph shows the dramatic drop in traffic after a negative SEO attack and the yearlong effort we undertook to help traffic recover.

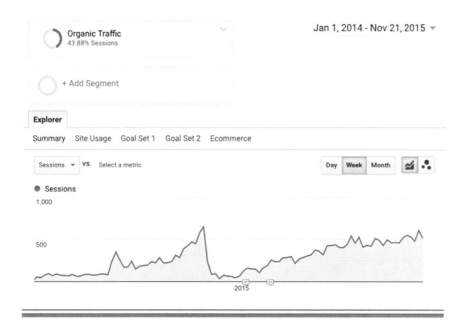

FindLaw Link-Selling Case

The FindLaw link-selling case demonstrates the value of links, the paid market for them, the (former) value of anchor text, and Google's response. In 2008, FindLaw aggressively marketed a product called SEM-C.[19] The "product" essentially was a purchased link program in which lawyers could leverage the domain authority of FindLaw by purchasing a set number of links and defining both the anchor text and target destination for those links. FindLaw specifically called out the SEO benefits of doing so in their marketing collateral: *"SEM-C includes articles submitted by the advertiser and hard coded links to be placed on the FindLaw Legal Professional portal. As FindLaw has a favorable rank with the search engines and is THE legal authority, customers will benefit from having a link on the FindLaw portal . . . Customers will have increased rank and penetration within natural search results on*

---

19. If you'd like to read the full, original product description from FindLaw, it can be found at https://mockingbird.marketing/wp-content/uploads/2018/06/FindLaw-for-Legal -Professionals-SEM-C-Product-Details.pdf.

major search engines." FindLaw's product sheet quickly came to the attention of Google's Webspam team, headed by Matt Cutts.[20] FindLaw's PageRank[21] subsequently fell dramatically.[22]

Part of Google's approach to combating link spam is a set of evolving guidelines, which can be found here: https://support.google.com/webmasters /answer/66356?hl=en. Although there currently are 13 separate items, I'll call out a few that are particularly common in the legal industry:

- *"Widely distributed links in the footers or templates of various sites."* This is extremely common among website developers, especially in the cutthroat legal marketing industry. Many legal marketing agencies will add a link to their site in the footer to their own benefit. For example, "Site by Law Marketing Super Expert Ninjas." These links not only violate Google's guidelines, but also enable competing agencies to identify who has built them.[23] Note that these footer links weren't originally called out as violations by Google.
- *"Keyword-rich, hidden, or low-quality links embedded in widgets that are distributed across various sites."* This stipulation initially was specifically added because a law firm was widely distributing a "hit counter"[24] across thousands of different sites that surreptitiously linked back to the . . . law firm. Like the footer links, these widget-based links have not always been on the black-hat[25] side of

---

20.   Cutts left Google and in 2016 joined the Pentagon's U.S. Digital Service (USDS), initially working for the Digital Defense Service under USDS.

21.   PageRank is a Google legacy term. Back in the early days of SEO, PageRank was Google's way of publicizing the authority of a given page. PageRank was a 0-10 score and published on the Google Toolbar. It was removed entirely by April 2016.

22.   Barry Schwartz covered this on Search Engine Land: Barry Schwartz, *FindLaw Hit By Long Arm of the Google Law Over Paid Links*, SEARCH ENGINE LAND (Aug. 27, 2008), https:// searchengineland.com/findlaw-hit-by-long-arm-of-the-google-law-over-paid:links-14637.

23.   This is one of the many reasons Mockingbird does not include a footer link in the websites we developer for law firms. At my agency, we have a healthy dose of paranoia on behalf of our clients and don't want to deliver a tactical pattern that's easily indefinable by other agencies that represent our clients' competitors.

24.   Hit counters were an old-school way of publicly displaying how many users had visited a site (that is, since the hit counter had been installed).

25.   "Black Hat" typically is used to describe SEO techniques that seek to work around Google's guidelines, while "White Hat" are SEO tactics that conform to those guidelines. Tactics that push the edge of Black Hat computing are predictably called Gray Hat. Think this can't get sillier? Think again . . . "Pink Hat" describes the technique of using female names or imagery to gain an advantage in SEO tactics ("I'm just a cute Pilates instructor named Honey, won't you please link to my website?").

Google's perspective. In fact, the original syndicated Avvo badge was designed with two objectives—the first to showcase a lawyer's score, and the second to provide a backlink to the Avvo SERP for that lawyer's particular practice area and geography.[26] It was specifically designed so that the anchor text to that target page could be changed and modified over time. Avvo is not the only site to deploy self-serving badges as a link-building tactic, but certainly pioneered the practice in legal.

- *"Links in . . . articles or press releases syndicated to other sites."* I include this because I continue to see lawyers duped into purchasing press release services based on the claimed SEO value.[27] Simply put, links on widely syndicated content (think press releases, or that news story carried verbatim by hundreds of different local newspapers) have no impact, because the volume of the links is a function of the syndication, not the quality of the content to which the many, albeit identical links point. In other words, Google computers are smart enough to recognize content verbatim duplicated across hundreds or even thousands of pages and deduce that links within those pages simply aren't editorially generated.

One of the tools created by search engines to manage the explosion of link spam is the no-follow attribute.[28] This attribute (coded as **rel="nofollow"**) originally was used at the page level and instructed search engines to crawl (or not crawl) (i.e., follow) links on a given page. However, the no-follow attribute is now applied at the individual link level. To understand the difference, imagine a great blog article with links that point to a variety of great sources in the blog post. Those links are valuable, editorial, and should be followed. However, the links in the inevitable comment spam that crops up on that page should have a no-follow attribute included. Overall, at best, this discourages spam; at worst, it strips the value of that comment spam link (which in turn preserves the value of the legitimate editorial blog links).

---

26. The badge actually had two links. The more prominent link was to the lawyer's individual profile page; the second almost hidden link was to the Avvo SERP.

27. A link-building tact masquerading as press releases have been pushed aggressively by press release companies who either know better or who are taking advantage of their ignorant customers. I wrote about this in 2011: Conrad Saam, *Public Relations: Link Building on Steroids*, SEARCH ENGINE LAND (Jun. 8, 2011), https://searchengineland.com/public-relations-link-building-on-steroids-75033. This useless tactic occasionally is connivingly marketed as "press release optimization."

28. Originally known as a "link condom" by early SEOs.

No-follow has been used (and manipulated) in a variety of ways. Turning off the no-follow attribute on lawyer profiles after the profile had been claimed was one way Avvo encouraged SEO-savvy lawyers to claim their profile. Most of the other legal directories have used a mix of follow and no-follow links to encourage advertising—i.e., advertise here and get a follow link to your website (fail to advertise and there's no link). This starts to blur the lines of editorial versus paid links. One of the many SEO scams foisted on lawyers was the mutual link exchange, with one of those domains no-following their links—essentially duping a "partner" into providing a follow link while stripping the value of the reciprocal link through the no-follow attribute.

Backlink Nuances: Geography

In the spirit of all links not being created equal . . . geography also comes into play. Simply put, a site in Milwaukee, Wisconsin, that is heavily linked from other business and organizations based in Milwaukee will perform better for searches in Milwaukee. This is especially true as it pertains to performance in Local Search (see chapter 3). For lawyers who are extremely active in their community, this is a great opportunity to build out a strong link profile. Coach a kids' basketball team . . . will the league link to your site? Deacon at the church . . . does that site link back to your firm? Organize a food drive . . . have the local press cover it and link back to your site. Many lawyers are extremely active in their community, yet they fail to have their online profile (specifically, backlink profile) reflect that fact. It's worth taking the time to sit down as a group and have every member of a firm chronicle their community involvement to uncover link-building opportunities.

Backlink Nuances: Relevancy

The other nuance around all links not being created equal is content relevancy. In this facet, sites that link to a firm that are topically relevant are more valuable than others. For example, a link to a law firm from the American Bar Association is much more relevant than a link from the American Medical Association (unless of course, the site is a medical malpractice site, in which case . . .)

The Fine Art of Link-Building

Links are the currency that determines success or failure in search results in the hypercompetitive legal industry. As discussed earlier, the competition for links typically is defined by a combination of geography and practice area—led by mass torts, personal injury, and then criminal defense. Building out a strong backlink profile takes time, ingenuity, and persistence. It also requires a long history of effort—in short, generating the links to define a highly authoritative site is a barrier to entry for newly formed firms. This may be unfair, but it's the reality of the SEO marketing channel.

Building backlinks often is one of most important but overlooked tasks undertaken by SEO agencies. Unlike the clear linear nature of technology platforms, or even content, backlink development is an uncertain art—part public relations, part technology, part luck, and part persistence. Additionally, as SEO agencies have constantly pushed the limits of link building, Google has responded by devaluing links from tactics that were formerly acceptable. In short, the available set of links that do have a positive impact on SEO performance continues to shrink. The following graph shows the dramatic impact of two advanced link-building campaigns Mockingbird undertook for a single client. Note the initial spike in traffic followed by an immediate and persistent increase in search traffic.

The first campaign was launched toward the end of 2015 and resulted in a persistent 29% traffic improvement. Following that campaign, the firm doubled down on its efforts the following year, which pushed traffic up by 83%. I use this example because it so clearly correlates backlink profiles with immediate and sustained SEO success.

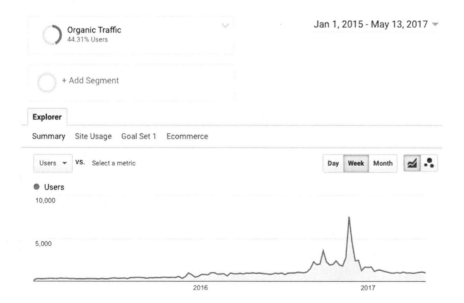

The simplest and most straightforward links for law firms to obtain are directory-based links. Note that these listings, which essentially are nothing more than a detailed lawyer profile, frequently live on extremely authoritative sites. Examples include Justia, Lawyers.com, Oyez, and lesser directories that have a modicum of domain authority, such as LawDeeDa. In addition, some directories are specific to practice areas, like NORML— that's National Association for the Reform of Marijuana Laws, which contains a (paid) lawyer directory that includes a valuable followed link. This obviously is a topically relevant link for criminal defense attorneys. More than a few enterprising entrepreneurs (and a smattering of agencies) have started their own directories, and the proliferation of these opportunities is somewhat comical. A good way to assess the value of a directory link is by assessing the domain rank (a score of external links that point to that domain) in tools like Ahrefs. In general, sites that have a domain rank less than 10 are useless and those with a domain rank over 20 are helpful. Many of these directory links are pay-to-be-included directories, making them technically in violation of Google's guidelines against paid links. However, the directories frequently get around this by "bundling" the link in with a set of additional value-added services.

Other link-building activities include using link research tools like Ahrefs or Moz to identify the backlink profile of competitor sites and trying to discern how those links were obtained. Guest posts—i.e., writing a blog on another business or organization's website—is another way to generate backlinks. An entire sub industry in the SEO space has arisen, with link brokers building relationships among publishers, authors, and editors to facilitate the placing of links; it's almost always a paid activity. With very mixed success, Google has gone out of its way to identify and devalue those links that are not really genuinely editorially driven.

The most difficult, genuine, and effective links are editorial links that are generated by good old public relations. PR drives links on highly relevant and extremely authoritative sites like the New York Times, local TV stations, authoritative subject matter blogs, etc. Despite their value, most SEO agencies have very little experience with PR (and PR agencies know next to nothing about SEO.) An aggressive, effective SEO agency will work in tandem with their clients on PR-driven link-building efforts, because those links make the fundamental difference in hypercompetitive markets like personal injury, criminal defense, and mass torts. Firms should look for news about cases they are involved in, current events that affect the legal industry, and salacious, celebrity-type stories on which they can weigh in through the media. Building relationships with local reporters is a painstaking, time-consuming, and long-term engagement. But when done effectively, it can make the difference between just playing in the SEO game and winning it. In city after city, we've seen that the dominant SEO player in personal injury frequently has the most prolific PR background, as well. The easiest case in point for me to cite is Avvo's initial launch. The integration between PR and link building was calculated, deliberate, and stupendously effective. Remember that in 2007, Avvo was a brand-new website. Yet, within a few short years, the company grew to (depending on who you ask) outpace old, established directory players like FindLaw and Lawyers.com. This growth was built on a PR-driven link-building campaign. When Avvo was sued just three days after it launched, we engaged in a proactive, aggressive PR campaign to defend it. The pitch to reporters was very simple: "new start-up rates lawyers and is predictably sued by . . . a lawyer." As I lined up interview after interview with a carefully researched list of high-level reporters who were eager to cover the story, I knew that each of their stories would include a backlink back to the Avvo domain. We expanded outreach to include what was, at the time, a small community of nerdy blogging lawyers who also wrote about the site (and linked to it). Within days, the brand-new, little domain had an enviable link profile that was responsible for driving traffic.

Preserving Authority After Website Updates and Domain Changes

One way that firms frequently torpedo their own SEO efforts is by unintentionally losing backlinks when they undertake a website redesign to upgrade their platform, or when their website moves to a new domain. Well-intentioned website upgrades can tank SEO performance when URLs change. For example, during a website redesign, the profile page URL for Bob the Lawyer may move from www.bobsfirm.com/bob to www.bobsfirm.com/lawyers/bob. Profile pages typically are a common destination for good links (like the local paper linking to Bob's great legal victory). Now, that link from the local paper points to a page on Bob's site that no longer exists. If you click through to that link, the resulting page is an empty error page denoted by a status code 404 (a 404 error). That link no longer holds value, plus, it makes the content on the website look out of date and unreliable. These URL changes can be more subtle—in our example, the simple addition of a / at the end of the URL, or the removal of www, or a move from http: to https:—all denote different pages. These broken-link problems are particularly common when firms migrate from one platform to another, because many platforms treat the way they generate URLs differently. So, changing platforms and moving from www.bobsfirm.com/bob to www .bobsfirm.com/bob/ can be all it takes to torpedo the value of your links.

To appropriately handle these changes in URLs and domains, you can use what is known as a 301 redirect to tell search engines that the content about Bob has moved. The 301 is known as a permanent redirect, and it does two things: 1) it seamlessly redirects any traffic from the old page to the new one, and 2) it tells search engines to update their indexes to reflect the new permanent location of the content.

On a more advanced level, a best practice is to ensure that a site doesn't have redirect chains. Redirect chains frequently are seen on long-standing sites that have been updated and "improved" many times. Consider if Bob's website had updated from Joomla to WordPress, later removed the www in the URL, and then went secure (from http to https). Bob's profile may have 301 redirected from http://www.bobsfirm.com/bob/ to http://www.bobsfirm .com/bob, and then 301 redirected to http://bobsfirm.com/bob, and then 301 redirected to https://bobsfirm.com/bob. These 301 chains do two things: 1) they make it longer (albeit just a little bit) to load the page, and 2) they may increase the number of URLs the search engine has to crawl. A best practice is to break the chains by redirecting each URL to the final destination with a single 301. (In this example, the 301s should each be replaced so they go directly to the current and final page. In Bob's case, he'll have multiple 301 redirects, but they are not chained—each iteration of his URL will have a 301 redirect directly to the current and final destination.)

This same issue appears, although on a much larger scale, when sites move from one domain to another, which can happen for a variety of reasons (although given the potential for errors, moving domains should be extremely carefully considered). Let's say Bob and Mary decide to merge their practices, and now all the content (and associated links) on Bob's website needs to be moved over to the new site (www.bobandmary.com). In the most rudimentary of errors, some designers simply start from scratch, copy the content from Bob's legacy site, and then paste it in the new domain. This is a tragically common error, and it wipes out all of the existing link value that Bob has accrued over time. Another common approach is to simply redirect Bob's entire domain to the homepage of the new domain—so, www.bobsfirm.com/bob now 301 redirects to www.bobandmary.com). This blunt-instrument approach does preserve the links; however, it loses the value of links at the individual page level. Links that used to point to Bob's profile page (helping Bob rank well for searches for his name) now just point to the homepage. The appropriate approach here is to redirect links at the page level. This is admittedly a tedious process, but it's a best practice. Also note that internal links (i.e., links on different pages on www .bobsfirm.com) need to be recoded to point directly to links on the new domain instead of creating yet another 301 redirect chain.

Over time, many firms have launched multiple websites—sometimes for different practice areas, sometimes for different locations, sometimes to add a blog as a standalone addition to a website, and frequently by an aggressively entrepreneurial attorney stymied by an unsophisticated or plodding IT or marketing department. This practice has been aggressively encouraged by self-serving vendors who make a living selling websites and blogs. From an SEO perspective, this multi-domain strategy is extremely foolish because it dilutes the overall volume and value of links that point to a website, making the site underperform in search results.[29] In pure economic terms, it's more than twice as expensive to market two sites than one because both the sites require link-building efforts. In addition, Google frowns on multiple sites representing the same firm showing up in the same search results. Multiple sites from the same firm competing for the same traffic is considered manipulative by search engines. For example, if you are researching "best mobile phones," Google doesn't want all of the results in the SERPs to be different domains owned and marketed by Apple. The same holds true for cars, accountants, t-shirts, and even law firms. Multiple sites also tend to confuse Local Search results (which company and which website is represented at this specific address?). Having said all that, there are some practice areas that are fundamentally contradictory that may happen to reside in the same law firm. The only client for whom we run a multiple domain strategy is very successful with both DUI defense and domestic violence—two practice areas that are thematically dissonant, and which probably shouldn't be represented in the same domain. One of the agency's most common tactics with a new client is domain consolidation. In domain consolidation, we take a firm's many domains and consolidate the content into a single, strong

---

29. Long before actually launching avvo.com, we considered launching with a massive multidomain strategy that had literally thousands of variants of www.DivorceLawyerNew Orleans.com, www.DivorceLawyerSeattle.com, etc. In the end, we eschewed this strategy given the stupendous link-building efforts that would have been required to make that work.

domain. The result invariably is a net increase in SEO across all the firm's content. This really is a case of 1 plus 1 plus 1 equals 5. Furthermore, frequently, we see increases in the more competitive content types (practice area pages), which see a boost from the enhanced backlink profile and need that authority to compete. A multi-domain strategy often is seen in stand-alone blogs. Given their less formal tone and timely content, blogs typically are fantastic at generating links. But sequestering them on a standalone domain separates the value of those links from high-converting content that drive's the lawyer's business—profile and practice area pages.[30]

In addition, as firms break up, merge, and start, the backlink profile of legacy domain is an asset that frequently is fought over. Simply put, it's very difficult to evenly split the backlink authority of a domain between two partners who have decided to part ways. I've personally found myself in the middle of three acrimonious fights over control of a domain. From a technology and SEO perspective, the "ownership" strongly rests with whoever registered the domain in the first place—be it the lawyer, the agency (FindLaw has a long history of doing this), or the front desk person of 8 years who we put in charge of the website because he was the only one in the firm under 35, so we assumed he'd understand technology, but who has long since left (we think to Australia), and we can't get ahold of anymore, because we never had his personal email address. Because of the value of domains, domain registrars are overly cautious and extremely persnickety about following rules and protocol when it comes to transferring ownership.

---

30.   For a counterpoint to this perspective, research commentary by LexBlog's Kevin O'Keefe, who adamantly insists that the intrinsic value of standalone blogs outweighs the SEO benefits of link consolidation.

3

LOCAL SEARCH

When marketers talk about Local Search, they are specifically referencing the mapped results that frequently show up on queries that have local intent. While a lot of this book deals with local marketing in general, this section of the book on Local Search deals specifically with those mapped results. To avoid any confusion, I'll always refer to this practice by the proper noun Local Search. The chapter delves into the tactical elements of how businesses become featured in Local Search, and it dives deep into elements law firms should focus on in highly crowded and competitive markets.

A (Brief) (Recent) History of Local Search

Local Search has evolved more significantly over the past three years than either of the other two primary elements of search marketing (Organic Search and Advertising). This evolution has been driven both by the location of where results are featured on the SERPs, as well as by the recognition of local intent among queries leading to more and more localized results. The net result: Local Search is now a major driving factor in generating business for law firms. We've seen many firms build their business by simply performing very well in Local Search without spending a dime on PPC or fighting in the Organic Search wars.

Before 2015, maps in SERPs typically (although not always) featured 7 different business results immediately below the ads with a small accompanying map on the right side of the SERP. This was usually referred to as the

7-pack. Variations were named based on the number of businesses displayed (i.e., 5-pack, 3-pack). In August 2015, Google began rolling out a revamped layout for results. Google enlarged the map significantly and moved it to be featured directly in line with the business results. Additionally, Google contracted the number of results from 7 to (almost always) just 3. This new 3-pack frequently is sometimes referred to as the Snack Pack.

While searchers can click to see more businesses, for the most part, those featured within that Snack Pack dominate. The importance of the Snack Pack was reinforced in early 2016 when Google moved ads from the right rail (on the right side of the SERPs) to be featured directly below the query box. Moving 4 ads directly below the query box pushed both local and organic results further down the page. Local Search's position above the organic results, combined with the new ads format, means that Local Search results are frequently the only unpaid results shown above the fold (i.e., without requiring scrolling to view).

On smaller, mobile screens, Local Search holds even more prominent screen real estate. In addition, Local Search results on a phone almost always include a functional phone number. This enables a prospective client to contact a law firm directly from the Google search results page without even needing to review the firm's site. From a conversion perspective, there's simply nothing more effective than a prospect holding a phone, wanting to talk to a lawyer, searching for a lawyer, and being able to talk to that lawyer with the simple touch of a finger.

Assumption of Location Intent

Another significant evolution in Local Search results is an increased presumption of local intent by search algorithms, even when there aren't Local Search words in phrase. Simply put, a query for "pizza restaurant" doesn't require "Seattle pizza restaurant" in a query to return mapped results for pizza restaurants in Seattle (assuming the user is running that search from Seattle.) Searchers are increasingly dropping the geo-modifiers in their queries as the search engines increasingly correctly anticipate that they are looking for local businesses.

In the legal industry, this has far-reaching implications because of the localized nature of (most) legal queries. Answers to informational searches (i.e., "what is the Blood Alcohol Content limit?") frequently are defined by state laws, so, we've seen an increasing volume of local business results generated by these types of informational, fact-gathering queries.

Note that because most laws that consumer-facing lawyers deal with differ by state, localized content between states can be very customized. However, localized content within a state can be very difficult to generate. In other words, because the laws governing divorce proceedings in Boston, Worcester and Dorchester are the same, it's very difficult to write genuinely unique content regarding divorce for these different cities in Massachusetts. Conversely, an employment firm with offices in Tennessee, Kentucky, and Ohio can write very genuinely different content for pregnancy discrimination in each of those three different states.

Local Search Tactics

The rest of this section is devoted to the tactical components that can literally put a firm on the map. Note that the Local Search algorithms are constantly changing and that the results themselves regularly rotate.

NAP: Name, Address, Phone Number

The cornerstone of Local Search is the consistency of firm's NAP (name, address, and phone number) across directories. Local Search algorithms look for a business to be listed exactly the same on Yelp as it is on the YP (formerly yellow pages), Citysearch, Google My Business, Avvo, and other directories. The reasoning is fairly simple: Google wants to ensure that when users use Google to find and then visit a business, the user actually arrives at the correct business. Google (and every electronic mapping service, for that matter) doesn't want to lose a user because they were erroneously sent to a law firm's old address.

The issue comes to light frequently with individuals at law firms, who break up and connect as frequently as junior-high dating relationships. Harrison P.C. becomes Harrison and More; which later transitions to Harrison More and Philips. Later, More, the firm's rainmaker, gets sick of Harrison, who he views as a leech, and strikes out on his own (with a new address and phone number) and the firm gets renamed H and P Law. Google's worst-case scenario is that their user is looking to speak with Bill More and uses Google to find and drive to H and P Law, only to find out that Bill is no longer there. That searcher doesn't get mad at Bill, or at H and P—the searcher usually gets mad at the search engine that sent him on a wild-goose chase. And he ends up looking for a new mapping service. Google has lost market share. To mitigate this scenario, Google looks for exact NAP consistency when putting a small business on the map. Barring that consistency, Google simply shows a different business.

As firms break up and attorneys move on to different firms, there is the potential for significant ethical and marketing problems. We have certainly seen some nefarious instances of firms deliberately manipulating Local Search to continue to generate business from prospects referred to their former employee. For example: "*Hi, Mr. More is unavailable right now. What can we help you with. . . .*" when More actually left the firm last February.

Search engines cross-reference NAP information across hundreds of directories. And they are looking for exact, verbatim matches—not Harrison and More, Harrison & More, or Harrison and More P.A. And this verbatim match continues to the address and phone number, as well.

Consistency with phone numbers is notoriously difficult for law firms. Tracking numbers (which are extremely important and covered in chapter 1) added to directories completely destroy NAP consistency. Additionally, many firms run two numbers—a local number and a toll-free 1-800 or 1-888 number. So, to be 100% clear: each office location should have one and only one phone number listed in directories.

Note that toll-free numbers are a relic of 1980s marketing. A toll-free number denotes a firm so successful [insert sarcasm], it could pay the per-minute phone call charges. The firm also probably successfully encouraged calls, for the extremely price-conscious prospects. However, it's been a decade or so in the United States since someone decided to make or not make a call based on the toll-freeness of said call. Today, with the exception of easily remembered, heavily branded (read: expensively marketed) versions, 1-800 numbers simply confuse both prospects and search engines. Firms who have successfully invested in developing the brand recognition for a 1-800 number should anticipate ongoing headaches with inconsistencies in their directory listings. This gets extremely complicated for multi-location firms for which the 1-800 number covers all of those locations. In this instance, best practice is for each secondary location to still have its own local number, and have it listed consistently across directories.

Tracking Phone Numbers and Directories

Chapter 1 highlights how tracking numbers work and why they are so pivotal in evaluating the efficacy of different online marketing channels. But, and this is extremely important, using tracking phone numbers in directories like Yelp, Citysearch, or YP generates inconsistent NAP listings. Imagine that a firm advertises on Yelp and wants to see how many phone calls that advertising generates.

So, the firm changes numbers to a tracking call number on Yelp. Now, the firm's Yelp listing contradicts its NAP on other directory listings, and the firm drops out of the Local Search results. Granted, if the firm keeps its true phone number in its Yelp listing, it won't be able to clearly evaluate the effectiveness of that Yelp ad placement. However, keeping its phone number intact on Yelp preserves the firm's position in Local Search. Accepting fuzziness in business reporting data instead of having solid data that confirms, "you aren't getting clients anymore" is a well-made trade-off.

All that said, Google now allows *two* numbers in the Google My Business listing—specifically, you can combine consistent NAP with a tracking number. For Google, this self-servingly highlights just how much business comes through these listings.

How NAP Gets (and Stays) Messy

Law firms are always surprised to see just how many directories they are listed in. There are literally hundreds of directories that are automagically populated by a handful of large directory listing databases. And one error, inconsistency, or legacy listing can be extremely hard to fix; it shows up across many different directories and is rewritten and overwritten by the large databases over time.

Fixing these directory listings requires contacting each directory, validating ownership of the business, and then requesting the change. This mind-numbingly tedious process is much more efficient through the use of tools from Yext and Moz Local, which automate some (but not all) of the work of managing listings. Note that you must use and monitor the tools on a consistent, ongoing basis—old listings and edited listings may inexplicably recur, and new erroneous data arises, creating a painfully tedious game of directory whack-a-mole. Additionally, we are seeing nefarious competitors changing vital data on law firms' listings to proactively knock them out of the Local Search results.

To check NAP consistency, use the free tools from Yext's Listing Scan (https://www.yext.com/resources/business-scan/) and Moz's unimaginatively titled Moz Local (https://moz.com/checkout/local/check). Note that these online tools look at different elements of local consistency. The tools complement each other and are not competitors.

An advanced tip is to run a Google search for a firm's phone number and business address to see what listings show up. Firms should do the same for old phone numbers and business addresses to see whether legacy directory listings are hurting their NAP consistency. Additionally, Google is looking for a real, physical address—not post office boxes or shared office spaces like Regus.

NAP and Legal Directories

Note that the tools from Moz and Yext manage large, generic directories, like Citysearch or YP. Neither tool has moved into vertical-specific directories. In legal, this means a manual outreach effort when dealing with NAP consistency in legal-specific directories like Avvo, Justia, and DUI.com.

Possum Algorithm Update

In September 2016, Google rolled out Possum, an algorithm update coined Possum by search nerd Phil Rozek. With Possum, while there were a variety of subtle changes to search results, one change had a major impact on a small section of the legal market: Possum changed Local Search by filtering out businesses that both shared an address and that were highly competitive with each other. Essentially, in the event of three personal injury practitioners working out of a shared office space, Google will now only show one of those businesses in Local Search results. Prior to Possum, all three attorneys might have been featured. The end result is more geographic diversity in the results displayed to users, but at the expense of attorneys and firms working in a legal office-share situation (and to the benefit of those who pay for standalone office space). This geographic diversity is explainable in terms of providing searchers with more variability in what they are seeking. There might be a reason why Mary doesn't like that building—bad parking, a bad part of town, or she might like to find another firm that is closer to her office or home, and so on.

Working from Home

Lawyers who work out of their homes must critically consider how (and even if) they want to have Local Search play in their marketing mix. This is especially true for some practice areas, like criminal defense. A prospect knocking on the door at 2 AM might not be extremely welcome. And while these attorneys frequently will use a local Starbucks as an "office," there really isn't an easy answer for how a home-office attorney can appear in Local Search if they want to keep their personal address anonymous.

Citations

Another component of the Local Search algorithm is the quantity and quality of structured and unstructured citations. A structured citation is a formal listing, usually in a directory like Yelp, Avvo, Google My Business, or YP. A structured citation contains standardized information in fields that identify the firm name, address, and other pieces of data, such as fax number. Unstructured citations are simply mentions of the firm without accompanying data; they show up in blogs and newspaper sites. An example might be a quote in the local newspaper from the managing partner or a listing of sponsors of the local little league team. Unstructured citations essentially are a measure of how frequently a business is being talked about. Just like backlinks, unstructured citations can vary by quality with elements of relevance (i.e., an attorney talking about a car accident for a personal injury firm), geography (i.e., the *Rappahannock Record* for a firm on the rural coast of Virginia), and overall authority (i.e., the *New York Times*, *Forbes*, etc., for anyone who can get it.) For example, we had one client whose California-based law firm received a major boost in Local Search traffic after one of its partners was quoted in various national newspapers regarding a news story that was completely unrelated to the practice of law.

Generating citations for law firms is similar to link-building—in fact, the two tactics frequently go hand-in-hand and often are conducted in tandem. Generating citations is a difficult, frequently creative, effort that combines PR (getting on the local news station), outreach (being active in the community), and sponsorships (donating to the local theater).

A strong citation profile used to be a primary element in what it takes to win in the Local Search SEO wars. However, Local Search nerds have noted a strong movement away from citations around early/mid-2018 and now see citations as being almost inconsequential.[1] In fact, the firms who have focused their tools on building out a network of citations mostly have moved on to other SEO tactics. An agency that pushes citations as a primary Local Search SEO tactic most likely is outdated in its thinking.

---

1. For more, read a conversation between two of Local Search's founding fathers, David Mihm & Mike Blumethal, *The History and Value of Citations, or Citations are Dead, Long Live the Citation*, STREETFIGHT (Jul. 22, 2019), https://streetfightmag.com/2019/07/22/the-history-and-value-of-citations-or-citations-are-dead-long-live-the-citation/.

Reviews

Customer-generated reviews of a law firm or of a specific attorney are a major factor in determining which listings show up in Local Search results. It's a pretty simple premise: Google wants to make its users happy. To do this, it's more apt to send users to businesses that generate a positive experience—an experience that is reflected in online reviews. Note that generating five reviews of a law firm is the basement threshold for triggering the review stars to show up in SERP results.

In most cases, it is wise for a law firm to encourage reviews of the firm itself as opposed to the specific lawyer the client worked with. First and foremost, consolidating reviews among the lawyers in the firm bolsters the strength of a single listing. Second, individual lawyers who have an extremely strong review profile on their personal Google listing possess a marketable and transferable asset. In an attorney-focused review, this is value for the attorney but not the law firm. In fact, it's an asset that's valuable to competing firms who are looking to lure that attorney away. Or that attorney may contemplate leveraging her glowing reviews to strike out on her own.

Best Practices for Generating Law Firm Reviews

There are a variety of automated tools and techniques that commonly are utilized to encourage reviews. Common sense dictates that client reviews for lawyers are extremely important, yet they are extremely difficult to generate. Very few people want to publicly cloud their Yelp restaurant and lawn service reviews with adulations of their creative DUI lawyer or exultations for their cutthroat divorce attorney. Our experience recommends the following best practices:

- Deliver a great product with great service. If you are an abrupt, unreachable, unprofessional, or incompetent jerk, your reviews will reflect it.[2] Attorneys frequently overlook this obvious golden rule of marketing. As legal search nerd, Gyi Tsakalakis has said, "you can't SEO your way out of bad service."

---

2.   My agency's legal clients who have the hardest time with Local Search tend to be unresponsive and obnoxious with us. These are characteristics that spill over from their approach with clients. That might be harsh, but it is (in general) true.

- Identify your clients who are truly thrilled. Don't be afraid to go back through your client list from the past 12 months to find clients who told you they were pleased with your work.
- Ask for the review. Accept that this is an awkward and uncomfortable situation, but ask for the review.[3] We have found that the best approach is for the attorney to ask in a face-to-face situation. That personal, spoken request is much more effective than a phone call, and email is simply far too easy to ignore for this admittedly uncomfortable and highly personal ask.
- Get some pro bono work and ask for a review. You deserve the recognition, adulation, and benefit of doing some great work in your community.
- "The ask": The right request is just like asking for a favor. Because that is what it is. "*I hope we have been of assistance to you in resolving your issue. It's our hope to help many people in a similar situation. If you could be so kind as to reflect your experience with us through an online review, I'd be most grateful.*" Note that state bar associations have struggled with the ethics of online reviews.[4] Additionally, Yelp specifically prohibits soliciting reviews, which is peculiar for a review-driven site.

There are a few caveats:

- Attorneys and law firms shouldn't review each other (mutual back-scratching).
- Make review management (i.e., monitoring, responding to, and requesting reviews) a systematic part of your experience.
- Don't review yourself.

---

3.   Keep in mind that lawyers provide an amazing service to individuals who frequently are at the end of their rope and facing their darkest days. These clients make fantastic, enthusiastic reviewers; preserving someone's access to their children is much more important than a perfectly cooked fillet mignon sautéed in an asparagus cream sauce and topped with a hint of bitterroot shavings.

4.   In my early days as the only marketing guy at Avvo, I spent an inordinate amount of time working with bar associations about the concept of lawyers being reviewed online. Many state bars were flummoxed, some were downright hostile (paging Florida—why, oh, why is it always Florida?). By now, most state bars have realized not only that consumers expect to be able to find user reviews of lawyers, but that these reviews actually serve to advance the general public's access to the legal industry. Note that each state bar has its own, evolving perspective on reviews. You are on your own to ensure compliance.

And never forget: A great review profile begins with delivering great customer service and great lawyering (two very different things that often are conflated to being one and the same).

Where to Get Reviewed

Lawyers tend to get wrapped up in wondering where they should ask their clients to post a review. The answer is simple: don't direct a client to a specific online review venue. Instead, realize that you are making a huge ask and that your role is to encourage the review without unnecessarily erecting any barriers to getting that review posted. Why push Yelp when your client already has a Citysearch account and a history of leaving reviews there?

Having said that, there are three major review venues that have a major impact for businesses:

- Google—Enough said.
- Yelp—Although very few prospects proactively search Yelp for a lawyer, keep in mind that 1) some still do, and 2) some search engines show Yelp reviews in search results for many different types of businesses, including legal.
- Avvo—One of the difficulties in generating reviews for the legal industry is the personal, confidential, and frequently embarrassing nature of many legal matters. Avvo is the only major legal review directory that provides users with a completely anonymous review forum. Also note that client reviews do not impact the Avvo rating, whereas lawyer endorsements do. Consider this the very important difference between a doctor's résumé and her bedside manner.

Responding to Negative Reviews

Earlier, we called out negative reviews as frequently being a symptom of poor service. In any case, it's not a matter of if, but when, a business will receive a negative review from an irrational, unhinged, or unrealistic client.

Guidelines for responding to negative reviews:

1. Respond. Remember that your response is an opportunity to market to everyone who reads the review, not necessarily the reviewer directly. This is a unique opportunity to demonstrate how much you care about your clients.

2. Respond to the review in person. Its easy (and cowardly) to be a bully online, passive-aggressively flaming a business from the safety of your living room and laptop. Consider countering this with a phone call, which adds a human element to the issue. Go into this call with your objective in mind: having the review removed or edited. Understand that your client is mad, offer to address the issues, and proactively bring up the review. Tread carefully here . . . your mileage may vary.

3. Don't be a jerk. Calling the reviewer a liar or an idiot, or intimating that they are a competitor reflects badly on you, not them (see rule #1).

4. Challenge. Challenge the review through the directory itself. Most directories have a process through which you can challenge reviews. After all, many of them live and die by the quality of review content, so they truly care.

5. Chill out. Consider waiting a month (or more) before challenging the review. Let the client cool down. Also, you don't want a review that's taken down by the site to further incense an angry ex-client. Minimize the likelihood of pouring more fuel on an angry or irrational client who hasn't had time to cool off.

6. Litigate? When dealing with reviewers, note that threats of litigation rarely do anything other than call more attention to the negative review—an online phenomenon dubbed the Streisand Effect. Section 230 of the Communications Decency Act (CDA) of 1996 provides publishers with legal cover to publish user-generated content like reviews without being forced to pull it down or divulge the identity of the reviewers. Note that more recently, both Section 230 of the CDA and publishers' refusal to reveal the identity of reviews have both been challenged in courts.

7. Don't be an idiot and violate confidentiality. It happens—don't be that lawyer.

8. Minimize the likelihood of negative reviews by delivering great service. Head off negative reviews by asking about (and resolving) any concerns a client may have prior to the end of your engagement. *"Was there anything we could have done better?"*

Local Search Spam

Given the business that's driven by local results, many law firms and shady marketing companies have started faking law firm addresses (local spam). Although we have seen examples in local spam across almost all legal practices, this practice is especially widespread among highly competitive practice areas like personal injury and criminal defense. One of the earliest documented examples of local spam originated in the legal industry, when law firms popped up on Google maps at the exact address of a train crash in California, the day after the accident.

The Three Major Types of Local Spam

1. *My Law Firm Is Bigger Than Your Law Firm (But It's Really Not)*

   In this example, a law firm falsely expands its geographic reach by pretending to have offices in cities or locations in which the firm isn't actually present. An obvious example of this is "shared" offices space, like that offered through Regus. More insidious is a post office box that masquerades as a fully staffed office. We've even seen a law firm's geographic footprint extend to a suite of car wash franchises (coincidentally owned by the managing partner's brother-in-law).

   Google, with its mindboggling access to smart brains, has gone to great lengths to combat these fake office listings and to *not* display them. Google knows full well the addresses of known office-sharing businesses and post offices. Google is getting better and better at distinguishing between real and fake offices through verification, manual checks, and a human reporting feedback loop.

   One mistaken perspective is that law firms can create distinct, multiple addresses simply by adding a suite number to an existing address. Contrary to popular misperception, Google does not take suite numbers into account when assessing the uniqueness of an address. You can't fake an office by adding a suite number to your law school buddy's standalone office in a town down the road.

Your Law School Roommate's Fake Office in Your Real One

An approach some firms have adopted to artificially expand their geographic reach is to have an office listing at a friendly lawyer's office in a practice area that doesn't overlap. These listings create multiple businesses listed at exactly the same address, and it completely ruins NAP consistency for both firms. Adding a suite number does nothing to clean up this mess. Essentially, Google doesn't understand which business belongs at that address and therefore, neither shows up on the Local Search maps. Experience a rapid and disastrous drop in your locally generated inquiries? It might be because when your law school buddy asked you whether it would be OK if he uses your conference room from time to time, he took your affirmation as carte blanche to generate innumerable directory listings that place his firm at your address.

2. *The Law Firm Named "Brooklyn Car Accident Lawyer"*

   Many firms change their "name" in the Google My Business listing to a keyword-stuffed name like Brooklyn Car Accident Lawyer (aka, Smith and Jones Law). Unfortunately, this keyword-stuffing has worked at driving local results, although it misrepresents the firm (check with your state on ethics issues, and check Google guidelines, as well). I strongly discourage this type of behavior. Firms who have changed their names to optimize for local have found their listings suspended, resulting in removal from the Local Search results for months at a time.

3. *The Non-Law Firm Law Firm*

   The legal market, being the competitive and lucrative market that it is, has seen the entrance of lead-generation businesses masquerading as law firms showing up in the Local Search results. Simply put, these businesses create Google My Business listings at fake addresses, along with phone numbers and a law firm–looking website. Once these sites rank in the Local Search results, if users call through, the phone is answered by an intake specialist, and the lead is then pitched to various real local law firms, who all pay a referral fee.

Dealing with Local Spam

Let's be crystal-clear about this: law firms and marketing agencies that deploy fake offices to show up on Local Search steal business from law firms who otherwise would have generated those clients. They cheat clients as well. We've seen attorney "offices" in Walmart, Kentucky Fried Chicken, empty fields, and run-down warehouses. Remember from chapter 1 that 43% of law firm clients chose their attorney based on proximity. With fake offices, the fundamental reason someone would choose to hire an attorney has been artificially constructed. This is no different than someone insisting on hiring a Harvard lawyer and being duped by a falsified diploma.

Stamping out local spam listings that have made it past Google's algorithmic filters is best done through a manual reporting feedback loop. Essentially, you report the false listing to Google. Anyone can report problems with a business listing via the Google interface. See the next image. For businesses that aren't actually present at the location, click the **Suggest an edit** link, and then follow the prompts from Google.

One of the realities of the crowded legal market is the extensive efforts undertaken by agencies and firms to fake office locations. This means that a simple manual reporting of spam may not actually affect the listing. Instead, you may need to go through an individual who has spent a significant amount of time building up a reputation in the Google Local community. This reputation is built by developing a history of high-quality edits to local listings. These people, frankly, have more sway in affecting listings than you might. In some cases, it is necessary to physically visit the alleged office location with a camera to document that the business is not there.

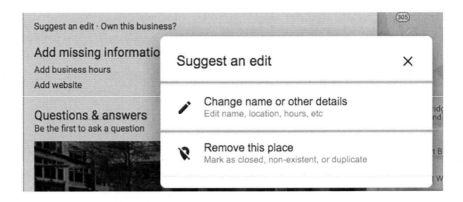

Note that in many cases, spam listings require ongoing monitoring and reporting; they tend to come back, like a rash. Spam listings most likely will reappear for months, or even years, as shady marketers continue to try to manipulate their results. Smart law firms (or their agencies) regularly monitor not just the three or four results that display in the initial local map, but also click through to the next screen and monitor the next 10 to 20 results for spam. Given the difficulty of managing local spam and its relative impact on a firm's business, it may be most effective to engage a reputable agency, one that has a highly reputable Google contributor on staff.

Additionally, it is very important to continue to monitor your own presence in local results, and to monitor the specific directory listings that drive those results. We have dealt with many examples of competitors or their agency representatives who repeatedly report legitimate law firm locations as being closed, or changing the firm's practice area focus in an attempt to remove a firm from the Local SEO map.[5]

---

5.   I consider myself a self-loathing marketer, and these types of disgusting tactics that have filtered into the legal marketing industry are one of the reasons why. I balked at publishing some of these examples because I don't want to be guilty of enabling more legal marketing shenanigans. If you engage in these tactics . . . shame on you, and know that state bar associations are starting to catch on. The Florida and Texas state bars are leading the way in taking action against firms who do these kinds of things. Mockingbird has proactively pushed for bars to do this.

4

ADVERTISING

There are innumerable marketing channels available to lawyers to spend their advertising dollars on. Some of them are valuable; many of them are not. The sheer volume of attorneys in the United States means that there are more advertising dollars chasing the same number of clients. The trick to generating a cost-effective advertising spend is to home in on the small but important differences that make your advertisement more effective than others. And remember that 43% of potential legal clients make their purchasing decision based on proximity. Tailoring an advertising spend to address this extremely strong consumer preference for local is frequently the key differentiator between a highly effective advertising campaign and torching your kids' college fund.

Remember that just because you are willing to drive across the state for that perfect, high-value case doesn't mean that your prospective client wants you to. She wants you nearby—down the road, across from the courthouse, next to her office. And it's what she wants—not what you are willing to do—that matters.

So, while there are many tactical ins and outs to advertising on various marketing channels—Avvo, Google Ads, Yelp, AdRoll—we are going to focus heavily on how to narrowly geographically tailor your advertising spend to what matters most to your prospects: your location in relation to theirs.

Advertising Payment Models

Before we get into the tactical side of advertising, it's important to understand the primary approaches to paying for advertising:

- Pay-per-click (PPC): Also known as cost-per-click (CPC), in this method, the advertiser pays only when someone clicks their ad. This is used heavily in search advertising through the Google and Bing Ads platforms. With PPC, the advertiser defines the highest price they are willing to pay for clicks generated from searches on a certain phrase, or keyword. That bid then competes with other advertisers. The higher the bid, the higher up on the page the ad displays, and the more likely the advertiser is to win that click. Note that the PPC model opens up advertisers to expensive click fraud—the practice of maliciously clicking on a competitor's advertisements to cost them money and drive them out of the market.

- Cost per thousand (CPM, for *cost per mille*): This is simply the price the advertiser will pay per one thousand impressions of an advertisement. This payment model commonly is used with display advertising (especially online banner ads), but it also applies to other mediums, like video ads.

- Cost per action (CPA): In this case, the advertiser pays only after a specific, defined conversion event occurs. This is used much less frequently in legal. Non-legal examples include filling out a bank loan application, buying fuzzy bunny slippers on an e-commerce site, or submitting an email address to a car dealership.

- Ad-free directory profiles: This approach is specific to small businesses. An advertiser can pay to clear competitor ads from its online profile in a third-party directory. The sales pitch is pretty simple: *"Pay us, or your competitors will be featured on your Avvo (etc.) profile."*

Search Ads (PPC or Google Ads)

Search ads (in which a user types a phrase in a search box and an advertisement that corresponds to that query appears in the search results) are the most common form of online advertising for attorneys. Formerly AdWords, Google rebranded its search ad platform as Google Ads in 2018 (strangely following Facebook and Microsoft naming conventions: Facebook Ads and

Bing Ads, now Microsoft Advertising).[1] Note that all concepts for Google Ads also apply to Microsoft Advertising.

As discussed earlier, PPC is a bidding system in which multiple bidders bid for the best position for any given phrase entered in a search query. The winning ads show up at the top of the Google Search results—there are three, usually, but sometimes four. Frequently, Google Ads also inserts an advertisement directly in the Local Search (mapped) results. By my estimation, the legal industry in the United States spends between $1.5 billion and $2 billion dollars annually on PPC ads.[2]

There are various elements that make up a PPC advertisement:

- Keyword—The phrase that is specifically searched by the user. Advertisers can use various approaches for specifying the keyword:
  - Broad match—The advertiser bids on any combination of words in a phrase. A broad match bid on "best Manhattan DUI lawyer" also triggers ads for the phrase "looking for great pro bono DWI attorney in NYC." Note that Google recognizes the synonym pairs "best" and "great" and "lawyer" and "attorney"[3]. In legal, Google's interpretation of a broad match has gone so far that they recognize firm names as being synonymous with the practice area. A search for "Smith Smith Smith and Jones" may trigger ads for other personal injury firms— even if those ads are bidding on generic personal injury keywords and don't specifically target the name of the law firm Smith, Smith, Smith, and Jones.
  - Phrase match—This is a much tighter targeting option, in which Google shows ads for queries that include the phrase in the order specified. From the earlier example, a query for "who is the best Manhattan DUI lawyer for expunging a criminal record"

---

1. Former search giant Yahoo previously had its own PPC platform; the most recent incarnation was called Yahoo Gemini. However, it has been phased out and Yahoo search is now driven by Bing's search platform.

2. This admittedly unscientific estimate is based on overall click volume, CPC rates, PPC market share information, and analysis of some of the financial documents of some of the larger legal-specific PPC vendors.

3. JDs have discussed ad nauseam whether to refer to themselves as lawyers or attorneys to optimize SEO. While this was a factor back in 2006 (it turns out people look for "lemon law lawyers" but for "estate planning attorneys" and "personal injury lawyers"). At this point, with its massive intellectual horsepower, Google has fully figured out that "lawyer" and "attorney" means essentially the same thing. Stop obsessing over this.

also triggers a phrase match-based advertisement, because that query includes the phrase "best Manhattan DUI lawyer."

o Exact match—This type of targeting shows only ads for a query that exactly matches the keyword. But, "exact match" also includes "close variants." So, a "DUI lawyer" query still shows ads for the keyword "DUI attorney."

o Broad match modifier—A broad match modifier search triggers ads when all of the words in a query are entered in any order. You can identify broad match modifier terms in the Google Ads interface by using the plus sign (+) in front of each word: "+best +DUI +attorney +Manhattan." Thus, our example would trigger ads for someone searching for "best DUI attorney working in Manhattan." In combination with negative keywords (see the next search option), broad match modifier is a strategy sophisticated advertising agencies use to provide increasing layers of specificity within the campaign setup, and to provide accurate data on exactly which terms trigger ads. Thus, a generic "personal injury" campaign has a subset for "car accident," which in turn has a subset for "whiplash car accident injury," etc.[4]

- Negative keywords—Keywords that specify that an advertisement shouldn't show up. Obvious examples include "pro bono," "free," and "low cost." Less obvious examples may include geographic locations in which the firm doesn't practice or practice areas for which the firm has no interest—"expungement," for example.

- The advertisement—Technically, this is a "text ad," because it contains copy and is comprised of three different components:

o Headline—The blue link that a user clicks.

o URL—The "final URL" is where the click lands. The final URL frequently is a long URL or includes tracking parameters. What the user actually sees in the ad is called the "display URL" or the "display path."

o Description—The description is unlinked text that's displayed below the headline. This has gotten increasingly larger over the years.

---

4.   You can learn more about broad match modifier at *Broad Match Modifier – Explained*, Colewood Journal (Sept. 10, 2015), https://www.colewood.net/blog/broad-match-modifier -explained/.

Quality Score

The Google bidding algorithm isn't a purely linear mathematical system in which higher bids simply outperform smaller bids. Instead, Google also calculates the "quality score" of a campaign. The quality score takes into account a variety of factors that ostensibly measure consumer satisfaction. Simply put, Google wants to deliver a great experience to its users so users continue to click those Google Ads. Elements that go into the quality score include:

- The relevance of the landing page and the advertisement to the query.
- The speed and security of the destination website. That is, Google doesn't want to send users to hacked or slow websites.

The quality score impacts the ultimate position of an individual ad. An ad that has a higher quality score appears above ads with lower scores. This means that the winning bidder may in fact not make the highest bid but instead deliver a better customer experience.

Note that Google utilizes historical data to help determine quality score. This means that brand-new advertisements underperform similar ads that have already established a strong quality score. This is one of the (few legitimate) reasons that agencies recommend longer-term contracts. In general, we recommend running a PPC campaign for no less than three months before you assess the efficacy of the campaign.

Ad Extensions

In addition to the standard text ad, Google displays a wide array of ad extensions that provide the user with more options and information about your firm. These ads significantly increase the on-screen real estate of the advertisement at zero incremental cost. These ad extensions are most relevant to the legal industry:

- Location
- Call
- Message
- Sitelinks
- Structured snippets
- Price
- Promotion

In general, Mockingbird configures its campaigns by using all these options, because Google tends to pick and choose which are actually displayed. Furthermore, the more ad extensions that are displayed, the larger the advertisement (at no incremental cost).

Bidding on Competitor Brands

A particularly aggressive PPC tactic is bidding on competitor brands. For example, Coke bids to advertise "Coke" when people search on "Pepsi," or Ford bids to show Ford F-150 advertising to people who are searching for "Chevy Silverado." This happens both deliberately (a law firm bids on the phrase "Smith and Jones," for example) and occasionally unintentionally (a law firm bids on the phrase "law firm," and its advertisement is triggered when someone searches for "Smith and Jones law firm").

Note that the advertisement itself may not be misleading. In the last example, the competitor law firm isn't actually pretending to be Smith and Jones; there's unintentional overlap in search terms that they *did* want to acquire. Google handles this by not allowing competitor terms to show up in the ad, even though a specific branded keyword triggered the ad. So, Coke can't say, "We are better than Pepsi" in its "Pepsi"-triggered ads, but it can have an advertisement that says, "Buy America's original cola." Very creative advertisers can use a firm's positioning against itself. For example, a Texas firm that was advertising against the well-known phrase "Texas Hammer of the Law" places an ad that says, "Don't get nailed" to people searching for "Texas hammer."

In general, the best approach to countering these brand-based ads is to bid on the firm's name and in the name of all the lawyers in the firm. These bids tend to be extremely low-cost (relative to most legal search terms). Additionally, the very high-quality score you get when you have the site that reflects your own brand (i.e., Coke.com is much more relevant to people searching for Coke than for Pepsi) relative to competitors means that the economics work out even better when you're bidding on your own brand. With the exception of heavy offline personal injury and criminal defense advertisers, these spends typically range from $20 to $50 per attorney per month and may be the very best marketing investment you can make.

Display Advertising

Display advertising is the deployment of visual banner ads that click through to a law firm website. Google's display network is massive, but the platform provides increasingly specific opportunities for targeting based on 1) the content of the specific site, and 2) the users. For example, a site about running most likely will show ads for Adidas sneakers instead of law firm services. It all depends on the targeting that's established for that campaign.

Facebook's Audience Network ads are display ads that can personalize advertisements based on both explicit and implicit information that's generated from a user's Facebook profile. Want to reach young moms in Wisconsin who like BMWs? How about people who play rugby, fly internationally on a regular basis, and really like marijuana? Facebook can find them for you. If you can define your audience, there's a good chance you can target the audience on Facebook. After that, it's only a matter of setting the right campaign goals and creating ads that capture people's attention as they scroll through their news feed. Note that in legal, these demographic audiences can be particularly difficult to identify. For example, there isn't a group on Facebook of people who "like" getting into car accidents.

Remarketing

Remarketing, also known as retargeting, is the online tactic that deploys display advertising that follows a user around the web. For example, if I'm browsing skis on REI.com today, I'm going to see ads from REI for those particular skis tomorrow and the following day when I browse on NewYorkTimes.com, OnlineGames.com, ESPN.com, and so on. Remarketing can be exceptionally cost-effective because you are placing your brand in front of someone who is already considering the firm.

Remarketing raises a variety of privacy concerns. For example, imagine a spouse discovering divorce lawyer ads or ads around specific medical issues that pop up in the web browser on the home computer. Accordingly, advertising publishers have rolled out a series of limitations for retargeting that focused on privacy. They called out personal issues, including medical and legal issues, as unacceptable targets for remarketing.[5]

This means that in most cases, remarketing for law firms is (at least, in theory) frequently is not allowed. Most remarketing restrictions are based on the entirety of the content on the target website. So, having a single page about divorce or injury may disqualify an entire law firm's website from remarketing. In practice, the enforcement and implementation of these restrictions has been haphazard at best; some legal sites have continued to be able to run remarketing. Should you find yourself in this latter category,

---

5. Google's restrictions on remarketing update constantly, and guidelines are published here: https://support.google.com/adspolicy/answer/143465. Also note that Facebook's remarketing content policies are much more liberal than Google's and offer much more opportunity, especially for the legal industry.

my strong recommendation is to continue doing so without revising the campaign so as not to inadvertently trigger scrutiny.

Directory Advertising

The websites lawyers love to hate . . .

The Martindale-Hubbell directory, a compendium of lawyers, was first published in 1868. Since then, these leather-bound tomes have proudly adorned the walls of law firms around the country. More recently, Martindale-Hubbell directory volumes frequently are featured as the uninspired backdrop of many lawyer profile pictures (*"I'm a lawyer; you know that because of all of these tan books with inlaid gold lettering on the shelf behind me."*). With the arrival of the Internet, these leather-bound tomes found themselves migrating to the web. This gave the general public access to lists of lawyer names, frequently via search engine queries. The first directory to truly master SEO was FindLaw, an online firm established by computer programmer Tim Stanley. FindLaw's genius was in taking freely available information, and then organizing and formatting it in a way that was accessible both to humans and computers. During the 1990s, FindLaw brought information about lawyers and the legal profession to the Internet-enabled population. For legal, this truly was revolutionary (although most lawyers wouldn't recognize this for another decade or more). Legal information was no longer bound on dusty bookshelves, but instead accessible to anyone with a dial-up modem and a computer. In 2001, FindLaw was sold to West Group. (After a short-lived relationship, Stanley and West Group parted ways in an acrimonious split.)

Directory Popularity Studies

Beware of studies that purport to crown the king of legal directories. Many of these studies are thinly veiled sales pitches commissioned by directories through dubious third-party researchers to "study" the market. They primarily are undertaken to bolster sales and marketing collateral. The most egregious (to the point of comical) example is Yelp, which commissioned the market research firm Nielsen to ask Yelp users whether they preferred to use Yelp for searching for a lawyer online. The study specifically excluded Google from the consideration set and, not shockingly, crowned Yelp the winner.[6] (This is why people hate marketers.)

---

6.   Read more at Emelina Berkshire, *Yelp Releases Nielsen Survey Data and Declares Itself King of Local Directories*, MOCKINGBIRD MARKETING (July 15, 2014), https://mockingbird.marketing/yelp-releases-nielsen-survey-data-declares-king-local-directories.

There are now hundreds if not thousands of directories that list lawyer information littering the web. Some of these are legal-specific (lawyers.com), some are generic (Yelp), some are local (Seattle Better Business Bureau), and some are relics of the phone books (YP). Recently, we've seen an increase in legal marketing agencies that build directories of their clients and then sell these listings . . . to their clients. Some of these directories have extremely deep pockets and are staffed by armies of tech-savvy nerds who fully understand the intricacies of SEO. Most are not, though, so approach most directory opportunities with skepticism and a grain of salt.

Strong directories, however, perform extremely well on three types of extremely high-value searches:

- **Name**—This is the original purpose of a directory—someone is referred to a lawyer and heads to Google to look for more information about "attorney bill smith."
- **Practice Area + Geo**—These are extremely high-value searches. For example, someone who was just in a car accident uses a search engine to get information about "Seattle car wreck lawyer." Note that the geo modifiers (in our example, "Seattle") are used with less frequency as users modify their behavior under the assumption that geographic location is taken into account by search engines.
- **Informational**—These searches are more research-based, but frequently will lead the user to hiring a lawyer. For example, "what is the fine for a second DUI in Mason County?" These informational searches are higher up in the sales funnel—the user is less likely to pick up the phone and hire a lawyer in the very near future.

Legal directories learned to monetize their success with search engines by placing advertising on highly specific pages on their sites. While there are numerous models employed, they all revolve around a central premise: "This user is looking for X type of lawyer in Y location; we have the capability to place ads from lawyers in Y who do X in front of that user." A directory that has detailed information about what practice areas individual lawyers engage in makes this monetization very easy. For example, if a user is looking at a directory profile of Bill Smith and the directory knows that Attorney Smith is a car accident lawyer in Evanston, Illinois, the directory can sell advertising on Smith's profile to other car accident lawyers in and around Evanston. Many directories, including Avvo, FindLaw, and Yelp, encourage lawyers to defend their own profiles by paying to keep their profile advertising-free. While this is not technically proactive advertising, it demonstrates the power of search-savvy directories. It also showcases one of the common emotive sales techniques that directory advertising sales staff use: fear that if you don't pay to clear your profile of competitor advertising, you'll lose those offline referrals who vet you online to competitors who advertise on the directory.

Over time, directories have consistently performed well in search engines for all three types of search results: Name, Practice Area + Geo, and Informational. Organic Search results on SERPs for all three types of searches showcase a mix of directories and lawyer websites. Anecdotally, directories typically account for 4 to 7 of every 10 Organic Search results. Directories typically are clustered toward the top, in the top 1 to 4 positions, followed by a smattering of law firm websites. Philosophically, this has always puzzled me. Google's driving goal is "to organize information and make it universally accessible."[7] Providing a user who is looking for a divorce lawyer in Atlanta with search results that are dominated by lists of divorce lawyers in Atlanta (which is all directories really are) instead of actual lawyers seems antithetical to this goal. A cynic might suggest that this is simply to drive more law firms to compete to appear on the page through advertising. A more balanced view sees this as Google deliberately displaying a mix of different types of information from which the user can further evaluate different lawyers.

Google has continued to modify and adjust SERPs in layouts that decreasingly feature Organic Search results. Go back just six years and organic results were shown at the top of the screen, with ads featured on the right rail. The top of the SERP is now dominated by three or four ads, followed frequently by a map of local business results (which currently contain one or two ads), followed eventually by the Organic Search results. This loss of screen real estate for Organic Search has had a negative impact on traffic to the directories (especially for high-value Practice Area + Geo searches, which the map almost always features). Having said that, many directories continue to generate a large volume of traffic. Overall, I see this restructuring of the SERP as a long-term detriment to directories overall.

---

7.   https://www.google.com/search/howsearchworks/mission.

FindLaw

After the sale of FindLaw to West Group and the breakup with FindLaw founder Tim Stanley, FindLaw expanded into an array of legal-related services, most notably, websites. FindLaw came under extreme criticism for its long-term agreements and one-sided contracts and became notorious for the practice of registering its own client websites for themselves—essentially owning the websites instead of building them for clients. In 2008, SEO veteran Todd Friesen exposed FindLaw's widespread link-selling program by using a black-hat technique expressly forbidden by Google's guidelines. FindLaw rebounded and now sells directory listings, directory advertising, and bundles of PPC-based advertising. It also continues to sell websites to lawyers.

Justia

Shortly after Tim Stanley's contentious departure from FindLaw, Stanley started competitor Justia. Justia lacks the name recognition of the big, established players, but it has an online footprint that frequently outperforms them. Stanley has continued with his initial mission of bringing freely available legal information to the general populace. The Justia legal directory powers two other strong directories: Oyez (www.oyez.org) and the legal directory of the Legal Information Institute at Cornell University Law School. Although neither of these directories feature prominently in search results, both of them offer lawyers a backlink from a highly authoritative domain (see chapter 2). This is an easy three-for-one opportunity for lawyers—Justia requires just a simple, albeit manual, verification process to confirm a lawyer's identity and standing as an attorney.

Yelp

Widely hated by lawyers (and almost all small business owners), Yelp continues to be important to the legal industry. The Yelp review engine powers listings that show up in branded name search results in many (non-Google) search engines. This is especially important because of the strong authority (warranted or not) given to Yelp's star reviews and the prominence of those stars in search results. While many lawyers believe Yelp is not a resource for people searching for an attorney, ignore Yelp at your risk. Note that Yelp's prominence in search results and user behavior is highly variable by city and region. In general, Yelp is most prevalent in younger, tech-savvy, and West Coast cities and almost immaterial in urban and sparsely populated regions.

Among the many things that engender acrimony toward Yelp among small business owners is Yelp's practice of filtering reviews out of results. This practice is grounded in Yelp's long-standing view that quality reviews are best identified by reviewers who leave a large volume of reviews. Power Yelp users are deliberately cultivated through the Yelp Elite program. The unfortunate result is that users who have left only one or two reviews often see those reviews filtered out. This enrages small business owners who deliver great service and convince their clients to sign up for Yelp to leave a first review, only to see that review effectively disappear.

For many years, Yelp sold advertising on an impression basis—pay X dollars for your ad to show up Y number of times. Yelp frequently also threw in the "ad-free profile" as a benefit. Given the extremely low volume of Yelp traffic for legal queries, the purchase amount for this advertising was typically very low. Having said that, it was still grossly overpriced. By comparison, pricing even for the expensive Google Ads was a relative bargain. Within the past two years, Yelp has moved to a PPC model for some of its advertising, and it now has some inventory in the legal market. In many markets, this has flipped the economics of Yelp entirely. Although there is extremely low inventory in most markets, that inventory can be purchased for extraordinarily low prices, because there's usually little or zero lawyer advertising competition. The biggest cost might simply be the logistics of setting up and then monitoring the campaign over time. Just don't expect more than one or two inquiries for your very low spend. Note that if you happen to do a lot of legal work in the restaurant industry, Yelp may be a great channel for you. Almost all restaurants are manically interested in Yelp and almost nothing else.

LexisNexis/Lawyers.com/Martindale-Hubbell/NOLO

Every industry experiences consolidation. Legal directories are no exception. The online holding company Internet Brands gradually swallowed up various legal players, including LexisNexis, Ngage (an online chat provider), and legal directories Lawyers.com, Martindale-Hubbell, NOLO, and in 2018, Avvo. Interestingly, as performance in the search results goes, many of these directory brands have seen their presence diminish considerably—specifically, Martindale-Hubbell and NOLO. Lawyers.com still has a reasonably strong presence.

Avvo

The Avvo web presence does not seem to have diminished considerably since its February 2018 acquisition by Internet Brands. Note that the Internet Brands business model frequently involves a focus on consolidation and efficiencies, and not on investment and innovation. Within months of the acquisition, 250 staffers at LexisNexis were let go;[8] likewise, Avvo's entire top executive staff left Internet Brands within months. In the case of the latter, I find this a sad state for the legal industry. While many lawyers and most bar associations took umbrage with Avvo, know that Avvo founder Mark Britton is responsible for accelerating the adoption of innovation and technology in the legal market during the mid-to-late 2000s. Under Britton's guidance, Avvo made huge strides in utilizing technology to make lawyers and the law much more accessible, in many different ways, to the common American. The Avvo website continues to perform moderately well in Organic Search performance—particularly in the extremely lucrative Practice Area + Geo search category. Most recently, Britton has joined Clio's board of advisors.

Avvo's Name and Doctor Detour

The Avvo name is a riff on the Latin word for lawyer or advocate—*advocatus*. The name was specifically chosen because it doesn't have an association among the general populace for the legal industry (i.e., not "attorneys are us," "law brain,"[9] or anything else identifiable as legal). This gave the budding tech start-up the flexibility to explore additional verticals in the future. Looking to become the "Yelp of professional services," Avvo launched in the medical field in 2010 by profiling and rating over 800,000 doctors. It was an ambitious, albeit poorly executed, extension of the legal brand that died less than two years after it launched. Part of Avvo's failure in the medical arena was its fallacious assumption that people look for doctors the same way they look for lawyers. Search engines are well-suited for the heavily researched, highly anonymous activity of looking for a lawyer. In contrast, most doctors are referred by other doctors, or they're contained in a small subset on an insurance company plan. Because of this, lawyers are aggressive, active marketers while doctors are, at best, apathetic and disinterested (with the noted exception of elective medical providers such as weight loss and cosmetic surgeons). This online marketing apathy made it extremely difficult for Avvo to engage doctors to contribute both free-form and profile content.

---

8.   Thomas Gnau, *LexisNexis to Cut 205 Positions*, DAYTON DAILY NEWS (Oct. 24, 2013), https://www.daytondailynews.com/business/lexisnexis-cut-205-positions-nationally/C3ImKaIXvDIfjgSa3pX3QK/.

9.   LawBrain was one of the original names considered for Avvo.

Super Lawyers

Bill White and Steve Kaplan grew Super Lawyers out of the Minnesota-based magazine *Law & Politics* in the early 1990s. The magazine's history is print, city-centric magazines with issues that feature the best professionals, although it also has an online component. Because of the magazine's prevalence, the Super Lawyers award has a greater brand recognition among the general populace than most other related awards. Super Lawyers was bought by Thomson Reuters in 2010.[10]

Directories and State Bar Associations

State bar associations ostensibly are the nexus of the most up-to-date and comprehensive information about attorneys. Theoretically, they should have been winners in the movement of lawyer content from books to the web. However, state and local bar associations simply lack the funds and technical know-how to compete with for-profit directories that are backed by Silicon Valley venture capital. By and large, prospective clients rarely turn to a state or local bar website to search for a lawyer.

---

10. For more about the interesting history of Super Lawyers, see Patrick Dunn, *The Origin of Super Lawyers*, SUPER LAWYERS (Dec. 12, 2017), https://blog.superlawyers.com /super-origin-super-lawyers.

5

WEBSITES

Websites obviously are the foundation of a firm's online presence. A well-coded, well-designed, fast website drives traffic, encourages inbound inquiries, and communicates a firm's unique positioning and message to prospects. Simplistically, website design and overall experience impacts conversion rates (the percentage of website visitors who contact a law firm) by roughly 30%.[1] A site that looks and performs like it was built 10 years ago immediately communicates to prospects that the firm either doesn't take itself seriously or that it can't afford a new site. Further, poor design can unintentionally obfuscate ways to contact the firm—for example, a phone number that's hidden in the footer. Conversely, an extremely well-designed site can entice and encourage prospects to reach out to the firm. We monitor all of our site redesigns to see how the impact conversion rates, and typically see a 3% to 8% improvement; although some extremely dated legacy sites have seen a conversion rate bump of more than 30%.

Law firm websites should display well both on desktop devices and on mobile devices through technology called mobile-responsiveness. Mobile-responsive means that the layout of the site dynamically adapts to different screen sizes. Google specifically penalizes sites that don't do this—the user experience is terrible, and users have to zoom in and out and squint to see undersized text.

---

1. This number is completely unscientific and assigned to an assessment of a subjective element: design. However, it is directionally accurate and a helpful construct. I believe that poor design can drop conversions from the status quo by about 20%, and great design can improve conversions by about 10% over how a more typical site would perform.

Great design encourages prospective clients to reach out to the law firm in the way that is convenient to the prospect. We've already discussed the four conversion approaches (phone call, text, chat, and form fill). Great website design incorporates all these approaches without obnoxiously pushing the "call now!" message. Many designers and marketing experts insist on adding a "call to action" on each page. These invariably manifest as text slapped onto the end of the practice area content. For example, "*If you or someone you know has been in a Seattle car accident, you should hire a Seattle car crash lawyer. Call the Law Offices of Murphy now at. . . .*" Let's be serious for a moment. The "call to action" in this case is the presence of the phone number, a form fill, *and* a chat functionality incorporated seamlessly into the site's design. I'm not sure there are any prospective clients who are so stupid that they need to read text that instructs them to contact you.

Other design elements encourage inquiries by visually conveying expertise and authority. The most prevalent of these are third-party badges—the Avvo badge, Super Lawyers, Million Dollar Advocates Forum, etc. In the design industry, these are known as "trust marks," and frankly, they're unrecognizable by the vast majority of prospective clients; they just communicate authority. Predictably, not all trust marks come from reputable sources. For example, Lawyers of Distinction, based in Florida, purports to represent the top 10% of lawyers through a rigorous personal vetting and background check process. In reality, anyone with an email address can purchase the "award" for an annual fee of roughly $700.[2]

Website Speed

One of the major factors of website success is site speed. For Organic, Local, and Paid search queries, Google simply favors sites that load quickly over those that take forever (as do consumers—in fact, much of what Google favors is driven by consumer sentiment). Speed has become

---

2.   For example, I applied for the Lawyers of Distinction award on behalf of my pet chicken, Zippy. Zippy was accepted, although she declined to pony up the money for the overpriced plaque and badge for her website. There are at least two dogs who have been accepted by the Lawyers of Distinction. I single out this company not because it is the only one, but because it is the most brazen. You can read more here: Conrad Saam, *Lawyers of Distinction Scam: Cease & Desist Threat*, MOCKINGBIRD MARKETING (Jan. 4, 2018), https://mockingbird .marketing/lawyers-distinction-cease-desist-threat; and Conrad Saam, *Lawyers of Distinction SPAM (Plus a Lesson on Useless Traffic)*, MOCKINGBIRD MARKETING (Feb. 23, 2018), https:// mockingbird.marketing/lawyers-of-distinction-spam-and-a-lesson-on-useless-traffic.

a major ranking factor in organic, local, and paid search performance, especially on mobile devices. There are innumerable factors that go into site speed, including the overall efficiency of the code, the hosting provider and location, and the actual content (for example, given their large file size, movies take a long time to load). A variety of third-party vendors assess a website's speed. In general, a page should load in less than two seconds; ideally, in around one second. But remember, this also is relative to the performance of competitive sites.

Website Design and Local

Done well, design is an opportunity to easily and immediately communicate a local element to a firm's practice. Big-box website provider Scorpion propagated the practice of using iconic local imagery as website homepage backgrounds to give their clients an immediate tie to a specific location. A backdrop of the Pike Place market immediately communicates Seattle; Faneuil Hall makes you think of Boston; a covered bridge brings to mind Pennsylvania's Amish country.

But a website can go even further than this in communicating *local*. There's an opportunity to show off a firm's history with a location—"*Jill grew up in Worcester, attended Boston College Law, drinks Dunkin Donuts coffee every morning, and cheers for the Patriots.*" The bio can showcase a firm's involvement in the community: "*Jill works at the Habitat for Humanity project in Dorchester*"; or her local reputation: "*Jill appears on the ABC Boston News.*"

Another way to communicate local is to feature a local phone number conspicuously (and continuously) incorporated into the site design. Vanity numbers and toll free 1-800 or 1-888 numbers tend to do nothing more than communicate to prospects, that the business might not be local. With the exception of truly memorable toll-free numbers (1-800-LAWYER, which was heavily marketed to retain that recall among consumers), toll-free numbers do nothing from a conversion perspective. According to a 2012 Marchex study, there was no difference in the numbers of calls placed to 1-800 numbers versus local numbers.[3]

---

3. *How Important Is a Local Phone Number*, MARCHEX, This study was published in 2012 but is no longer available on the web.

Phone Numbers and Mobile Website Design

Mobile website design should include what we've called a *sticky* phone number. This means that a phone number is always visible to the user when they are navigating the site. This frequently manifests itself as a bar at the top or bottom of the site that includes the local number. This very basic design element encourages inbound inquiries to a firm. This number must be functional—i.e., when you touch it on a mobile device, the device dials the number.

The Importance of Website Design

"Do I (really) need to pay for a website redesign?"

The look and feel of your website is fundamentally a conversion driver. Simply put, does the site compel people to take the next step with your firm, or does it dissuade them that you are the right person for their needs? Like it or not, this is one of those cases in which a book really is judged by its cover. Your legal prowess, education, abilities, background, connections, and knowledge all are (erroneously) evaluated based on the design of your site. In complex service industries, purchasers frequently are uninformed and unqualified to evaluate the quality of services—think, a knee replacement surgeon, a tax accountant, a . . . lawyer. In these cases, the prospect typically turns to third-party cues to help them evaluate the quality of a potential service provider. Harry Beckwith famously wrote about this in his book *Selling the Invisible*. In the book, Beckwith describes consumer preference experiments in which consumers repeatedly select oranges based on the orangeness of the fruit—regardless of the fact that color and flavor are completely uncorrelated in oranges. Simply put, a well-designed, modern-looking site that uses high-end custom photography is a very *orange* orange, and it encourages viewers to make the call or fill in the contact form. Conversely, a site that has a dated look and feel gives the same prospect pause when they are deciding whether to contact the lawyer. In rough (and admittedly unscientific) terms, design can have an impact on conversion from between –20% and +10%. That is, a site with a dated, simplistic, confusing, or cheap-looking design may turn off one in five prospective inquiries who might otherwise have contacted the firm. On the other hand, an exquisitely designed site, with custom photography and clear, differentiated messaging may increase conversions by 10% beyond what a standard, generic, big-box legal website would.

With the cost of website development projects ranging from $3,000 to the mid-$30,000 mark,[4] deciding when to update the look and feel of a website should be approached with a very simple business assessment: does the loss of business caused by a dated design (admittedly, this is a subjective question) exceed the cost of updating the site by a factor of 2 or 3? In business terms, this is a simple assessment of the likelihood that an investment will generate a 100%–200% ROI. If the answer is no, firms should invest their money elsewhere—typically, in driving more traffic to the site, instead of creating a flashy and modern site visited by no one.

An element to consider in this assessment is traffic volume to the site. A firm should consider overall traffic when it decides how much it wants to invest in the design of its site. Improving the conversion rate by 2% on a site that gets 10,000 visitors a month probably will pay off well. But if you have a site with a paltry 100 visitors a month, it will take the firm a lot longer to recoup an investment in the site's redesign. Put another way, highly trafficked sites can afford to spend more on exquisite custom design because the sheer volume of traffic will lead to that much more business (the ROI argument). Here are some very round numbers: roughly 3%–5% of lawyer website visits generate an inquiry through phone, chat, form fill, or text.[5] A well-configured reporting infrastructure for a site should be able to calculate the inquiry-to-traffic percentage for that specific site. If that number drops well below that rough 4%, perhaps a dated site design is the culprit. The business analysis for engaging a site design requires two estimates:

- How much can I increase my conversion rate?
- What is my close ratio when people do contact me? (Take into account that not all inbound calls are inquiries from prospective clients—they may be the pizza delivery guy looking for directions, opposing counsel calling regarding a matter, or yet another PPC vendor wanting to schedule a dog-and-pony pitch.)

Using the assumption of a minimum of a 100% ROI, back-of-the-napkin math says that the increase in revenue must be more than twice the cost of redesigning the site.

---

4. American Bar Association Benchmark Study: Conrad Saam, *Law Firm Website Costs*, LAW TECHNOLOGY TODAY (May 20, 2016), https://www.lawtechnologytoday.org/2016/05/aba-benchmark-study-law-firm-website-costs.

5. Conrad Saam, *SEO Traffic Generates 1 Call Per 30 Visitors*, MOCKINGBIRD MARKETING (Aug. 8, 2016), https://mockingbird.marketing/seo-traffic-generates-1-call-per-25-visitors.

Custom Photography and Website Design

One of the most cost-effective ways to create a high-converting, highly polished, slick, personalized site is to employ a talented local photographer. Upgrading visual content from stock imagery to custom shots enables lawyers to let their personality come through visually. A talented photographer will eschew the classic lawyerly poses (man in a tie in front of leather-bound books, mahogany conference room with green reading lights, scales of justice, Greek columns) and instead communicate a personal brand through photography. Additionally, local photography that incorporates iconic local scenery, buildings, etc., immediately communicates a notion of *local* to a site visitor. To communicate location, we've used a picture of a trio of lawyers crossing the Chicago River, a drone flyover of a law firm's office nestled in a southern Utah canyon, a lawyer at Camden Yards, and one of the many iconic covered bridges for a Bucks County law firm. My favorite lawyer image is of Robert Stone, solo practitioner and president of the Alaska Bar Association, in a "hero image" shot of him in camouflage in front of his small plane on a glacier outside of Anchorage. There are simply no words that can communicate genuine Alaskanness compared to this picture.

Website Platform and the Popularity of WordPress

The underlying code on which a website is built is known as the platform. The most popular platform among law firms and many other sites by a wide margin is WordPress. Other publicly available website platforms include Joomla and Drupal. Originally developed as a blogging platform, WordPress has evolved into the standard website platform. The overall consensus is that WordPress is the easiest to use, and it's extensible (it's easy to add different layers of functionality to). The relative ubiquity of proficient WordPress designers and developers makes it easy for a law firm to make changes, adjust content, and update its site. This puts the control of the site in the hand of the law firm, not their agency.

Some law firm–specific vendors have developed their own proprietary platforms, including Scorpion, Foster Web Marketing, FindLaw (although even FindLaw is moving to WordPress), and Lawlytics. The primary concerns with these proprietary platforms are twofold. First, it's difficult for a small cadre of developers to keep up with changing technology compared to the thousands of WordPress-based developers who contribute to the code base. This means that proprietary systems often lag in performance. A well-coded WordPress site will almost always outperform a proprietary platform. In the following image, we see a whopping 44% drop in traffic when a firm moved from WordPress to Scorpion's proprietary platform.[6]

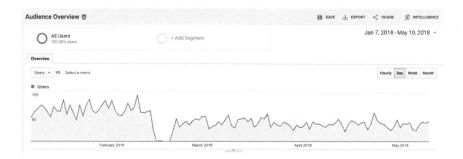

Second, proprietary platforms can tie the firm to its vendor. Want to add a page for a new lawyer? Call and pay the vendor. Want to upgrade your homepage imagery? Call and pay the vendor. Proprietary platforms self-servingly make it difficult to switch agencies because the only people who can work on, or even access, the back end of the site work for that specific agency. In addition, migrating away from a proprietary platform is techno-logically difficult. Moving from a different website platform can add $1,000 to $4,000 to the cost of upgrading to WordPress. In contrast, changing from one WordPress agency to another is simply a matter of adding a new user account. This puts control of the site in the hands of the law firm, which is where it should be—not with the agency.

Hacking WordPress and Managed Hosting
A well-deserved knock on WordPress is that its prevalence has made it a widespread target for hackers. We've seen this over and over again—law firm websites end up unwittingly hosting porn, pirated movies, and even low-end dating pages by being hacked. The main problem for law firms with a site that includes porn and movies (or porn movies, in some cases) is that Google no longer thinks the site is being about car accidents. Instead, according to

---

6.   I share this data to help you visualize the ramifications of proprietary platforms that simply can't keep up with the pace of change required to compete in the legal market. The result is poor performance.

Google, the site is about something entirely different. Dealing with a hacked site can be either simple or hard, depending on what has happened. In some cases, we have had to rebuild the entire site from scratch. To mitigate against hacking threats, WordPress developers constantly update the software, and some website hosting companies now provide what is known as managed WordPress hosting. Among other things, a managed host will 1) disallow certain unsecure plug-ins on the site, 2) automatically upgrade to the latest non-beta version of WordPress, and 3) make and store a daily backup of the site, so that if it does get hacked, the solution is simply to reinstate the site from the day before the site was infected. There are a handful of high-end managed WordPress hosts. The market leader in legal is WPEngine, and while the cost is greater than run-of-the-mill hosting providers, the peace of mind that comes with running a managed site is worth the incremental cost. To date, we've never had a site on WPEngine hacked in a way that we couldn't easily recover from.

6
SOCIAL MEDIA

This very small chapter deliberately sequestered at the end of the book focuses on the actual practice of social media marketing—engaging with individuals via social media platforms. This is not to be confused with using social media as an advertising channel, which is covered in chapter 4, along with a discussion of advertising.

This book's chapter on social media marketing is intentionally very small. Despite all the promises and proclamations by self-anointed social media marketing experts, gurus, ninjas, and mavens, in general, social media as a direct-to-consumer marketing channel for the legal industry is ineffectual. The reasons are very simple. First, in most cases, legal issues are extremely personal, private, and frequently embarrassing concerns. It's rare to come across a person (and I'd argue, a terrible client) who will announce his third DUI on Twitter, or a wife who shares via Facebook that she just found her husband in bed with the nanny, or a mesothelioma victim who wants to share pictures of his kitten with a lawyer via Instagram. Second, both the effectiveness and the ethics of social media ambulance-chasing—picture a Twitter reply that says, *"I saw you posted that you were in a car accident"*—are very much in question.

By and large, lawyers have grossly overinvested in social media marketing consultants and experts. This is exacerbated by the fact that social media makes an empty appeal to a lawyer's ego with easily quantifiable metrics. *"I just crossed 2,500 Twitter followers!"* or *"The firm got 17 more likes on Facebook with our photo campaign of Halloween kittens in pumpkins!"*

obviously fail as empty metrics because kittens in pumpkins have zero correlation with the need for a lawyer in a given geographic market and practice area. Furthermore, most contributors of likes, thumbs-ups, retweets, pluses, as well as "friends" and "fans" don't remain actively engaged with a social media profile unless that profile is actively managed. In other words, the individual who "liked" your firm's picture of a kitten in a pumpkin 14 months ago probably is not going to remember the name of your firm if he is involved in a car accident today (turns out the dude just really, really likes kittens).

Despite my overall skepticism of social media marketing for the legal industry, there are some lawyers who understand how it really works and use it to great advantage. Social media is extremely effective in establishing and fostering relationships with others, albeit only with others who also happen to be active on social media. Because these are interpersonal relationships, they require time, attention, and a personal connection. The key here is that social media requires a time investment and a genuine, engaging interpersonal relationship-building mindset. It also requires a love of, or at least a comfort with, technology. Tech-savvy extroverts (and at the risk of painting with a broad brush stroke, the Venn diagram overlap with the typical lawyer profile for this is admittedly small) can do very well on social media—identifying and building relationships with key influencers, referral sources, the local press, etc. Additionally, because the foundation of social media marketing is genuine relationships, it takes time and attention to nurture and grow a social media marketing strategy, just like with in-person relationships. Expecting results right off the bat just because you posted a photo of a kitten in a pumpkin on your new Instagram account is simply foolhardy. Done well, at best, social media is a flywheel that takes 6 to 18 months of proactive nurturing and attention to start generating momentum. And by proactive nurturing, I'm talking about a daily commitment to generating content and interacting with individuals on a one-on-one basis.

A fantastic use of social media is taking advantage of its inherent ability to humanize lawyers. Most prospective customers are eager to see the person behind the suit and the JD. Yet, most law firm marketing collateral goes out of its way to ensconce the individual in typical lawyerly trappings. Due to its much less formal nature, social media can really showcase a lawyer outside of the lawyer costume . . . hanging out with her kids, riding a mountain bike, eating out at a great local restaurant.

Instead of reading further about social media, I'd counsel law firms to look to the example of Morris Lilienthall, one of five lawyers in the Huntsville, Alabama-based Martinson & Beason. Morris is a great example of both how to do social media marketing right, and of the long-term time commitment required to make it work. In Morris's own words: "Social media is how I outcompete much larger firms in my market—they have the dollars, but I put in the time in the community, and that has made all of the difference."[1] Mo's social media profile discards the lawyer costume entirely and has little, if anything, to do with the law or (directly) generating clients. He shares videos of his weight-loss regimen, photos of his kids, and his experience with the March of Dimes. He also runs short-form interviews with prominent local personalities, such as the head coach of the local hockey team. He also spends a large amount of time interacting with people who make comments and ask questions. But it's clear through all of these tactics that Mo isn't fishing for clients or even building a brand—he's leveraging the reach of social media to connect with people on a personal level. And as his engagement and connections continue, his reach in the Huntsville, Alabama, market slowly but surely expands.

The key here is that social media marketing is a conduit for building relationships that may turn into business over time. And because these are interpersonal relationships, they cannot be outsourced. Done well, social media is a reflection of the firm's or the lawyer's engagement in their real-life community. The social media marketing "expert" masquerading as his lawyer client on Facebook is a surefire path to the eventual awkward real-life conversation that looks something like, "*Hey Bob, what a surprise to bump into you at Smitty's Restaurant. I really like that post you wrote about the impact of Trump's tariffs on the local orange growers.*" When not only did Bob *not* write or even post the article, but he's never seen it, and he has no idea what the perspective is. Plus, he has no idea who this guy at Smitty's is, because he's never seen the profile pic that accompanies the Facebook profile. Awkward. This is a classic example of a wasted—perhaps even counterproductive—investment in social media consultants. The focus on interpersonal relationship-building means that it is extremely hard (I'd say foolhardy and misguided) to outsource social media marketing to a third

---

1.   A direct quote from Morris, in one of my many conversations/debates with him regarding the right approach to community and social media marketing.

party. Doing so is the functional equivalent of uploading a doctored picture and hiring a "consultant" to chat for you on an online dating site.

Finally, many firms outsource to social media experts the task to "*get our posts up on the social media sites.*" This extremely wasted manual effort can be replaced by website plug-ins that automatically post a new blog post into Facebook, Twitter, etc.

Social media is a fantastic way to humanize the lawyer behind the firm, which is a key element in the hiring decision behind many prospective clients. Typical lawyerly imagery hides the personality of the individuals in a firm— dark suits, red ties, formal pictures, and mahogany desks do little to show any personality. Social media offers an appropriately casual opportunity to show off who you are: a loving parent, active in the church, a fisherman, an avid cyclist, engaged in the Black Lives Matter movement, an avid foodie who frequents (and reviews) local restaurants. Further, much social media sharing is inherently local, offering an individual the opportunity to both engage with the local community and to showcase offline engagement— "*Here's me coaching the kids' hockey team,*" "*here's me on the local hiking trail,*" "*here's me at my office on Main Street across from the courthouse.*" Some argue that this casual sharing is not befitting for a law firm, and that lawyers should segregate their personal and professional personas online. From a marketing perspective, nothing could be further from the truth. In a crowded service-based industry, "*this is who I am*" is the easiest and most important business differentiator. Lawyers who don't utilize social media to easily and quickly deliver that personal positioning become just another JD among a sea of lawyers in a prospect's eyes.

If you are going to take the time to invest in the social side of social media, invest heavily. And invest your time, instead of your money, in marketing "experts." The key here is to engage, engage, engage, without asking for or even expecting anything in return. There are a variety of tools you can use to identify key influencers (other people online who have a wide reach) with whom you should deliberately engage. Obvious targets include local press, local politicians, business owners, athletes, and finally . . . potential refer- ring attorneys (many of whom are represented on social media via "con- sultants," so *caveat emptor*). In the Morris Lilienthall example, Lilienthall profiled local police officers, the owner of a local brewery, a local DJ, the president of the local MADD chapter, and city councilmen. He also has used the platform to (only occasionally) build his network among people in the legal industry through online interviews of legal authors and national legal association leaders. Through all of this, you'll never hear Mo say something along the lines of "*if you've been in a car accident, call. . . .*" It's simply not the point of social media done right. But it can be the end result if you invest the time and effort to genuinely build relationships online.

If you are considering jumping into the social media marketing game, I'd make two strong recommendations. First, ask yourself whether you are genuinely both extroverted and tech-savvy (or at least tech-comfortable). Would you be eager—not just willing—to experiment with your iPhone to self-film a video and then figure out how to use low-cost or no-cost software to do basic post-production—add audio, an intro screen, and perhaps a watermark? Two, give yourself a six-month commitment window, and then follow a very regular practice of posting content and engaging with the community. If you can't match Mo's cadence, social media marketing may not be the right channel for you.

7

CONCLUDING THOUGHT

Marketing can ruin everything.

In the final throes of finishing this book, I found myself going back and forth with my ABA editor in what became a heated exchange about the book's title. In the end, she sent me the following email, rejecting the brilliant, creative title I had finally landed upon after hours and hours of pontification: "Since the metadata that goes to retailers like Amazon indexes the main title and subtitle separately, publishing SEO best practices favor main titles that concisely convey the substance/appeal of the book." Here's my editor using publishing SEO best practices to reframe the title of my labor of love: "Law Firm Online Marketing and the War for Local Clients: Making Your Address Work for You"—a mouth-garble of keyword-stuffed buzzwords intended to maximize book sales. And utterly devoid of interest, intrigue, soul, and appeal.

Let your great marketing simply be a reflection of great lawyering, and never let the marketing tail wag your law firm dog. Put differently, it's much easier to market an amazing product than an average one. You need to *be* that great product. Stay committed to being an amazing lawyer. Return phone calls quickly. Speak in layman's language. Show empathy, courage, and commitment. This is the first step in great marketing, and no level of expertise in SEO, PPC, or social media can replace it.

Having said that, extremely effective marketing increases demand for your services beyond what's needed to merely keep the lights on. Effective marketing enables you to become increasingly selective in the clientele you work for, or focus on the practice areas you're interested in, or raise your rates, or aggressively expand your firm's geographic reach. This book is a detailed tactical guide to help you reflect your great lawyering with great online marketing.

Kelly Chang Rickert, a lawyer and stupendously successful marketer, says, "I love all my clients. I handpick them." Great lawyering and great marketing makes this possible.

GLOSSARY

301 redirect Code that permanently moves the location of a webpage from one URL to another.

404 A status code error that indicates a broken webpage.

API A set of functions and procedures that allow the creation of applications that access the features or data of an operating system, application, or other service. For our purposes, this is the way different reporting systems can share data with each other.

Bing Microsoft's answer to the Google search engine. Today, Bing also powers Yahoo search (and advertising).

Bounce rate The percentage of sessions that visit one page on a website and then leave.

Call-only ads Online advertisements featured on mobile phones in which the user's only possible action is to call a firm directly.

Channel General marketing parlance for a specific marketing activity that drives results. This gets confusing and frequently is used interchangeably by marketers because it can apply both to a type of advertising (TV) or to a specific advertising spend (such as TV on Channel 9). In Google Analytics, "Channel" refers to the type of advertising (email versus Organic Search, for example).

Click fraud The practice of maliciously clicking on a competitor's PPC advertisements to cost them money and drive them out of the market.

Conversion Generically, an action you want a user to take. For law firms, this means contacting the law firm as an inquiry—specifically, a phone call, form fill, chat, or text message.

Conversion rate The percentage of users who ultimately contact a law firm. Varies widely by marketing channel.

Crawl Describes a computer program finding and "reading" webpages on the web by following links.

Crawl budget The number of pages a spider will crawl on a site. Essentially, a "budget" that is driven primarily by overall authority profile.

Direct (aka direct load) Users who go directly to a website by entering the domain in the browser or through a bookmark.

Dynamic call tracking A conversion-tracking approach whereby users from different marketing channels see a different phone number, which is then forwarded to a firm's primary number. The caller ID information is collected and associated with the marketing channel from which the phone call was generated.

Google Ads   Google's search marketing platform; formerly called AdWords.

Google Analytics   A free program from Google that tracks the online metrics of a website's performance. Should be the nexus of any law firm's reporting infrastructure.

H1   HTML code that defines the primary heading (H1) of a webpage.

Indexed   Describes a webpage that Google puts in the consideration set for showing up in search results.

Local Search   The results that show up in the mapped section of a search results page. Typically appears right below the advertisements for searches that have a high geographic intent, like "pizza restaurant." Most legal queries that have a transaction intent (i.e., "hire a divorce lawyer") include these Local Search results.

Long tail   Describes the mathematical reality that search is dominated by extremely specific queries and not by simple searches like "accident lawyer." The "long tail" relates to these longer, less frequently searched keywords that in aggregate make up the majority of the search volume.

Meta description   A set of short sentences that summarize what a webpage is about. Shows up on SERPs, directly below the clickable title tag.

Multi-channel attribution   An analytical technique that's used to evaluate the effect of multiple marketing channels working in combination to eventually drive a conversion. For example, a user first runs an SEO query, and then clicks a Bing ad, and finally calls after reading an insightful email from the firm.

NAP   The name, address, and phone number for a small business.

Natural Search   See *SEO*.

No-follow   Code that tells search engines to *not* follow a link; essentially, it strips the value of the link from an SEO perspective.

Organic Search   See *SEO*.

Pageviews per session   Pageviews divided by the number of sessions.

Pageviews   The number of pages viewed by all visitors during a specified time frame.

Parameter   A string at the end of a URL that is preceded by a question mark (?). The string can have a variety of influences on the page (from tracking to changing a sort order). For our purposes, parameters are where UTM codes reside for tracking purposes in Google Analytics.

PPC (pay-per-click)   Technically, a way advertisers pay for their ads—i.e., they pay a specific, predetermined amount only when someone clicks the advertisement. This is pervasively and inaccurately used interchangeably with "Google Ads."

Referral   In Google Analytics, a user who clicks to a website from another website.

SEO (search engine optimization)   The art and science of combing a website's content, authority, and technology to maximize exposure in the SERP. Frequently called Organic Search or Natural Search, it often is inaccurately used to include Local Search results.

SEM (search engine marketing)   A confusing catchall that describes all marketing tactics that are related to search marketing—specifically, Local Search, Natural Search, and Paid Search.

SERP (search engine results page)   The result of a query on a search engine.

Session   A set of actions from a single visit to a website.

Sitemap   A list of all the pages on your website that helps search engines find them.

Spider   A search engine program that follows links across the web to discover new content. Also used as a verb.

Title tag   The title of a webpage. The title tag also is what displays as the link in the SERPs.

UCR (useless content ratio)   The percentage of a law firm's pages that generate no traffic over a long time frame. Used as an indicator to evaluate overall content strategy, as well as content quality.

User   An individual person who is viewing a website. Occasionally referred to as *unique user* or *UU*.

UTM   Tracking code that Google Analytics uses to identify how traffic reaches a website.

WordPress   A platform that's used to build a website and manage the site's content over time.

Yoast   A common SEO plug-in for WordPress. In inexpert hands, can create more problems than it solves.

INDEX

Note: Page numbers with n indicate footnotes.